School Violence in South Korea

Seunghee Han

School Violence in South Korea

International Comparative Analysis

 Springer

Seunghee Han
MO, USA

ISBN 978-981-16-2732-3 ISBN 978-981-16-2730-9 (eBook)
https://doi.org/10.1007/978-981-16-2730-9

This Springer imprint is published by the registered company Springer Nature Singapore Pte Ltd.
The registered company address is: 152 Beach Road, #21-01/04 Gateway East, Singapore 189721, Singapore

*To my parents for their support
and encouragement*

Introduction

An Overview of School Violence in South Korea and Around the World

School violence is prevalent among students worldwide. International data from more than 50 countries showed that approximately 43% of elementary school students reported being bullied at least once, and 14% of students reported being bullied weekly (Mullis, Martin, Foy, & Hooper, 2017). Another international survey data revealed that approximately 23% of students reported being victimization at least few times a month, and about eight percent of students reported being bullied frequently for the same period in the Organisation for Economic Co-operation and Development (OECD) countries. While physical bullying is less frequent, being made fun of (14%) and having rumors spread about them (10%) are more common forms of bullying among students in OECD countries. Compared to OECD countries, South Korea (hereafter Korea) is one of the countries where its frequency is relatively low. Less than 10% of students in Korea responded to eight statements about bullying victimization (ranging from 1% to 9%), when the average % age of victimization in OECD countries ranges from 6% to 23% (OECD, 2019). A Korean national online survey data showed that elementary school students are three times more likely to be bullied than secondary school students, and verbal abuse and exclusion are the most common forms of school violence (Ministry of Education, 2019). While the frequency and forms of bullying incidents vary by region in Korea, more than 40% of students in Seoul reported being victimized at least once in the past year, and bullying, physical attack, or harassment are the most common violence toward students (Yi, 2013). In addition, more than 30% of elementary school students in five large cities in Korea reported being involved in a form of school violence (Kwon, 2012). Overall, serious violence including physical attack and sexual assault decreased over the past years, but cyberbullying has continuously increased in Korea (Ministry of Education, 2019).

Although international data shows Korea with fewer student victimization than their counterparts in other countries, there are still many students experiencing violence and are bullied in Korea. The Korean government has continuously reformed and implemented school violence prevention policies to promote a safer school environment. In 2004, the Korean government initiated an antibullying law in a multiple-year plan that emphasizes protecting victims and providing education to offenders as well as support rigorous research on school violence (UNESCO, 2017). In 2012, a significant reform for school violence prevention policies resulted from multiple bullying suicide incidents in Daegu. Eight students committed suicide after being severely bullied by peers in 2012, and those incidents occurred only for six months. Since then, a total of 14 students killed themselves from being bullied in just two years (Chu, 2013; Kim, 2011; Oh, 2013). Such horrid incidents shocked the entire Korean society and alarmed the government to initiate a prompt policy reform adding more strict antibullying policies, called Comprehensive Measure to Eradicate School Violence (CMESV). The policies stress school staff and parents' responsibilities for students' behavior, an improved school violence report system, promotion of sound school cultures through peer activities, encouragement of parental involvement, and Internet game addiction prevention (Kim & Oh, 2017; Office for Government Policy Coordination, 2012).

In this chapter, what we can learn about the school violence phenomenon from an international perspective is addressed. For the comparison of school violence in Korea, two countries, Japan and the United States (hereafter U.S.), were chosen for their shared similarities and differences in demographic background, education system, and economic position. In addition, Korean education system is influenced by Japan during colonial period and is developed by modeling U.S. education system. Most importantly, all three countries initiate school violence prevention policies and make great efforts to promote safer schools.

The purpose of this book and its chapter outlines are presented as follows.

Adoption of Comparative Studies

International comparative research is one of the most important research methodologies in social science studies including the field of education. Results from international comparative studies provide valuable, deeper insights and useful information for problem solving on the matter. Cross-cultural studies allow us to have fresh viewpoints on the issue and identify similarities and differences on the issue among different countries. In addition, it allows us to classify gaps of knowledge on the issue in multiple countries and directs us to problem solving from new perspectives (Kosmutzky, 2017; Hantrais, 1995).

School violence is a common issue around the world. However, its frequency, forms, definition, cause and prevention strategies vary across the globe. Comparative research methods are particularly useful for a better understanding of school violence. School violence might be defined in a broader way in certain cultures, and students, parents, teachers, and school principals might perceive it more seriously in some countries than others. School violence occurs in various forms and to a more severe degree in particular countries. Prevention policies for school violence might be harsher in some countries than others as well. When we examine school violence in a single country, it is easy to assume existing concepts, theories, and policies as reasonable. To expand our knowledge on the school violence phenomenon, we need fresh viewpoints and new approaches. Comparative views on school violence from different education systems, cultural backgrounds, and demographic backgrounds guide us to more questions and further development of ideas, allowing us to gain a deeper insight on the issue.

This book attempts to compare school violence in Korea with Japan and the U.S. The Trends in International Mathematics and Science Study (TIMSS) is used in this book as TIMSS is one of the most comprehensive and well-designed collection of survey data encompassing information from students, teachers, and schools from over 50 countries. The TIMSS data collection is started by the National Center for Education Statistics (NCES) in 1995. Data has been collected every four years since then, and the TIMSS 2015 data was the most recent record as of the start of this research.

Conducting a large-scaled secondary data analysis like TIMSS provides great benefits for international comparative research. We can simplify educational issues by drawing common conclusions across datasets. To ensure such advantage, it is important for international comparative data to assure valid instruments and assessment processes across the board, eradicating translation issues and standardizing survey procedures for all the countries. The TIMSS survey questionnaires are thoroughly examined and translated to minimize any cultural bias in assessing educational topics and terminologies. Procedures for the TIMSS data collection have been administered in close collaboration with the national center of each participating country (Chudgar, & Luschei, 2016; Strietholt, & Scherer, 2018).

Utilizing secondary data analysis is especially advantageous for descriptive analysis. In this book, frequencies, trends, and characteristics of school violence will be compared among Korea, Japan, and the U.S. by employing the TIMSS data and descriptive statistics. Findings based on adequate data and analysis methods will help school teachers, principals, researchers, and policy makers gain a better understanding and new insights on the issue of school violence.

Purpose and Outline of the Book

The purpose of this book is to provide information about school violence in Korea from an international perspective. Japan and the U.S. were chosen for the comparison because these two countries share similarities as well as contrasting features in terms of demographics, educational systems, and economic position. Utilizing quantitative research methods, school violence, and various factors including national characteristics, perception of various stakeholders, school characteristics, and school principals', teachers', and students' factors were investigated and compared in Korea, Japan, and the U.S.

Conceptual model on school violence is presented below (Fig. 1).

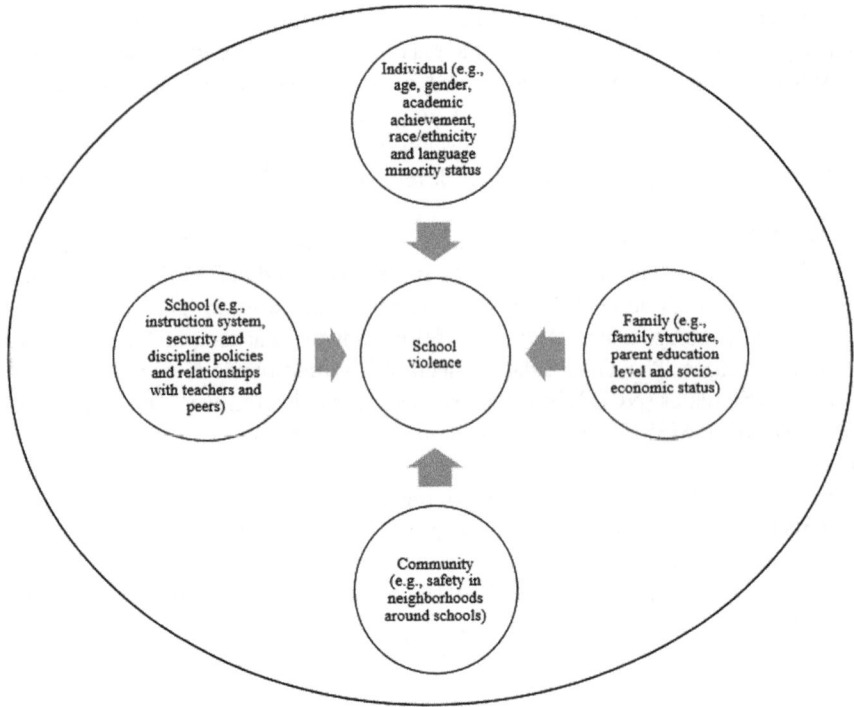

Fig. 1 Conceptual model of school violence

This book is composed of seven chapters. In Chap. 1, the definition of school violence is presented based on policy and legal documents, empirical studies, and how school violence is viewed by different stakeholders and in different cultures. Characteristics of Korea, Japan, and the U.S. are briefly presented for a better understanding of the demographic, educational, and economic aspects of each country. Statistics on school violence in the three countries are presented based on the results of national survey data and empirical studies. Specific research questions and research methods of the book are also addressed.

In Chap. 2, school violence as a problem in Korea is addressed based on previous studies and major news articles. Frequency and types of school violence in Korea, Japan, and the U.S. are addressed and compared by analyzing the Trends in International Mathematics and Science Study (TIMSS) 2015 survey data.

Chapter 3 presents school violence perceived by various stakeholders including students, parents, teachers, and principals based on intensive literature review. Stakeholders' definitions of school violence, reactions to school violence, and strategies to prevent school violence are addressed for each country.

Chapter 4 addresses school violence with demographic characteristics, economic circumstances, and educational system in the three countries.

Chapter 5 presents literature review on school characteristics and school violence and examines how school characteristics differ between schools with low- and high-level school violence in the three countries based on the TIMSS survey data analysis.

Chapter 6 shows individual and family characteristics and school violence based on the literature review, and student and family characteristics and school violence are compared by analyzing the TIMSS survey data.

Finally, Chap. 7 addresses policy approaches to school violence in the three countries and provides findings and lessons from this book. Policy recommendations and suggestions for future research are presented.

This book can be distinguished by two unique features. First, there are limited books on school violence in Korea published up to date. Furthermore, published books address school violence in Korean cultural and historical contexts by using qualitative methods and take conceptual and theoretical perspectives. Generalized patterns of school violence and associated student, family and school characteristics based on the national samples can be better investigated using quantitative methods rather than qualitative methods or conceptual research. Second, no published book examines school violence in Korea from an internationally comparative perspective. By comparing Korea to Japan and the U.S., this book will reveal the school violence phenomenon affected by each different educational system and cultural and social contexts, adding up to fulfill an identified gap in this research. This book will help us gain a better understanding of school violence in Korea and offer insights to develop preventative policies for educators and policymakers across countries.

References

Chu, C. (2013). Teen's death spurs call for action against bullying. *The Korea Herald*. Retrieved September 14, 2020, from http://nwww.koreaherald.com/view.php?ud=20130313000936

Chudager, A., & Luschei, T. F. (2016). The untapped promise of secondary data sets in international and comparative education, *Policy Research, Education Policy Analysis Archives, 24*(113), 1–16.

Hantrais, L. (1995). *Comparative research methods*. Social research update. Retrieved September 14, 2020, from https://sru.soc.surrey.ac.uk/SRU13.html

Kim, E. (2011). Middle school student commits suicide after talking with home room teaching telling her she was a wangtta. *MBC News*. Retrieved September 14, 2020, from http://news.naver.com/main/read.nhn?mode=LPOD&mid=tvh&oid=214&aid=0000199392

Kim, N., & Oh, I. (2017). Analysis of stakeholders' perceptions of zero tolerance policy for school violence in South Korea, *Journal of Educational Policy, 14*(1), pp. 61–78.

Kosmutzky, A. (2017). A two-sided medal: On the complexity of international comparative and collaborative team research, *Higher Education Quarterly, 72*, 314–331.

Kwon, D. K. (October 14, 2012). 30% of children used violence against colleagues at school: survey. *The Korea Times*. Retrieved September 14, 2020, from http://www.koreatimes.co.kr/www/news/special/2012/10/139_122182.html

Ministry of Education (2019). Statistics on school violence 2019. Retrieved September 14, 2020, from https://moe.go.kr/

Mullis, I. V. S., Martin, M. O., Foy, P., & Hooper, M. (2017). PIRLS 2016 International Results in Reading. Retrieved from Boston College, TIMSS & PIRLS International Study Center. Retrieved September 14, 2020, from http://timssandpirls.bc.edu/pirls2016/international-results/

OECD (2019). *PISA 2018 Results (Volume III): What school life means for students' lives*, PISA, OECD Publishing, Paris, Retrieved September 14, 2020, from https://doi.org/10.1787/acd788 51-en

Office for Government Policy Coordination, (2012). Comprehensive Measure to Eradicate School Violence. Retrieved September 14, 2020, from http://www.opm.go.kr

Oh, K. (March 20, 2013). *Korea struggles to save students from bullying*. The Korea Herald Retrieved September 14, 2020, from http://www.koreaherald.com/view.php?ud=20130320000605

Strietholt, R., & Scherer, R. (2018). The contribution of international large-scale assessments to educational research: Combining individual and institutional data sources, *Scandinavian Journal of Educational Research, 62*(3), 368–385.

UNESCO (2017). School violence and bullying Global status report. Retrieved September 14, 2020, from http://unesdoc.unesco.org/images/0024/002469/246970e.pdf

Yi, W. (2013). 40% students suffer from school. *The Korea Times*. Retrieved September 14, 2020, from http://koreatimes.co.kr/www/news/nation/2013/01/113_128451.html

Contents

Chapter 1
Background of School Violence in Korea, Japan, and the U.S.

This chapter provides basic framework about how to address school violence in Korea, Japan, and the U.S. throughout the book. School violence is measured in many ways. Based on literature, definitions of school violence are addressed and explained on how this book defines and measures school violence. For a better understanding of the cultural context for each of the three countries, distinct characteristics of Korea, Japan, and the U.S. are compared as well as statistics on school violence in each country. Finally, research questions and methods are explained by data analysis with descriptions of each chapter.

Definition of School Violence

School violence is defined in many ways as school violence has various forms and occurs both in physical and cyberspaces, and privately and publicly. In addition, school violence damages victims physically, socially, and emotionally, and its negative consequence can last until adulthood. School violence is perceived differently by different stakeholders and by offenders and victims as well as under different cultural contexts (Ireland & Ireland, 2003; Wrighta et al., 2017). In this chapter, definitions of school violence are presented based on previous research studies, policy documents, and legal documents.

In Korea, according to School Violence Prevention Law (*hakgyopokrekye-bangbub*), school violence is defined as any behavior causing physical, mental, and property damage to students in and outside school including physical injury, assault, threat, confinement, theft, defamation, insult, forced errands, sexual assault, exclusion, cyberexclusion and cyberbullying (Korea Ministry of Government Legislation, 2020). School violence has many different forms and one of the most common forms is bullying. In Korea, "*wang-ta*" is the word for "bullying," and it literally means "exclusion." Originally *wang-ta* is a shortened version of the phrase "*wang-ttadolim,*"

© Springer Nature Singapore Pte Ltd. 2021
S. Han, *School Violence in South Korea*,
https://doi.org/10.1007/978-981-16-2730-9_1

which means extremely isolated or excluded person. The term is used interchangeably with "*gipdan-ttadolim*" *or* "*gipdan-gorophim*," which mean being isolated from the group and being harassed by a group. Both terms refer to the offender as a group rather than an individual (Kwak & Lee, 2016).

According to the United Nations Educational, Scientific and Cultural Organization (UNESCO), school violence can be defined in three categories: physical, psychological, and sexual violence. Physical violence includes physical attacks, fights, or bullying and corporal punishment. Psychological violence includes social exclusion, emotional or verbal abuse, and psychological bullying. Sexual bullying includes unwanted touching, committing or attempting non-consensual acts, sexual harassment, and sexual bullying. (United Nations Educational, Scientific and Cultural Organization, 2019). In this version, school violence is defined with the focus on damage to the students themselves rather their possessions (e.g., having something stolen) and whether those violent acts are involved with weapons, drugs, or alcohol. Additionally, the setting of the violent acts, whether it is an incident of cyberbullying or assault on the walk back home from school, is not specified.

One of the major U.S. national surveys on school crime and safety defines school violence as "actual, attempted, or threatened fight or assault," and the types of school violence include threats of physical attack (with or without weapons), physical fight or attack (with or without weapons), theft, robbery, possession of firearms, distribution, possession or use of illegal drugs, alcohol, sexual assault, rape, and hate crime (U.S. Department of Education, 2020). School violence is not limited to the incidents that occur within school hours or premises. The scope of school violence expands school property and includes time on the way to or from school as well as school-sponsored events (National Center for Injury Prevention and Control, 2016). On the other hand, youth violence is defined as violent acts committed by young people ages 10–24 that use physical force or power to threaten or harm others intentionally and includes bullying, fighting, threats with weapons, and gang-related violence (Centers for Disease Control and Prevention, 2020).

Researchers measure school violence using multiple forms of violence: group bullying, verbal assault, physical abuse, forced errands, robbery, sexual harassment, and cyberbullying (Kim, Kim, & Kim, 2016), being involved in physical fights, feeling unsafe, and carrying a weapon (Sugimoto-Matsuda, Hishinuma, & Chang, 2013), physical attacks, stealing, name calling, sexual abuse as well as other bullying behaviors (Kwak & Lee, 2016). While there are similarities in the definitions of school violence, some researchers differentiate school violence from aggression. Bushman et al. (2016) define school violence as aggressive behaviors causing physical injury or death, yet spreading rumors is classified as an aggressive behavior rather than a violent behavior in their study.

In the research area, bullying is a more frequently examined form of school violence, and research on bullying has dramatically increased over the years. The number of publications regarding bullying increased about six times more from 2001–2005 to 2011–2015 (Smith, 2016). Researchers define bullying as "repetitive aggressive behavior with an imbalance of power" (Smith, 2016), "aggressive behavior triggered by external stress" (Tam & Taki, 2007), "aggressive goal-directed behavior that harms another individual within the context of a power imbalance" and emphasize three factors: goal-directedness, harm, and power imbalance (Volk, Dane, & Marini, 2014). The Olweus Bully/Victim Questionnaire, internationally well-known bullying self-report survey, defines bullying in seven forms including verbal bullying, social exclusion, physical bullying, spreading rumors, stealing or damage another's items, threatening, and race-related harassment (Olweus, 2006).

Under different cultures, the definition of bullying behavior shares similar concepts, terms and conditions, such as "intentional harm done to someone by another or others in some position of relative power" (Smith, Kwak, & Toda, 2016) and "behaviors whereby on student perpetrates an attack on another student(s) that produces emotional and/or physical suffering" (Dussich & Maekoya, 2007). In Japan, the Ministry of Education, Culture, Sports, Science, and Technology defines bullying (Ijime) as the "continuous physical and psychological aggression inflicted upon someone weaker, which causes serious pain on the victim...aggression that occurs both inside and outside of school" (Akiba, Shimizu, & Zhuang, 2010). European countries tend to define school violence in a broader way than in the U.S. European countries view school violence as any harmful behaviors where a perpetrator damages the victim physically, morally, or emotionally—anything that creates feelings of disorder through school climate and insecurity (Klein, 2012).

Different stakeholders, such as principals, teachers, students, and parents, might have different views on school violence. Offenders and victims also view school violence in their own ways. Researchers found that offenders define bullying differently in contrast to definitions in literature. While bullying is often considered as "repeated behaviors," offenders consider a single incident as bullying behavior. They also do not consider bullying behavior as always a result of imbalanced power between an offender and the victim (Ireland & Ireland, 2003).

In this book, school violence is defined as any behavior that causes harm to students emotionally, physically, socially, and mentally, as well as damage to someone's belongings. These behaviors are considered both offline and online. In addition, school violence in the book is primarily focused on victimized students rather than school staff or an outsider's victimization on school property. Offline victimization (e.g., cyberbullying) rapidly increases among adolescents (Bae, 2017; Lee & Shin, 2017) thus cybervictimization will be discussed in the book. In the analysis, school violence is measured using multiple items based on students' and school principals' reports (also used in the Third International Mathematics and Science Study (TIMSS) survey). For students' reports, nine behaviors are considered to measure school violence: (1) made fun of me or called me names, (2) left me out of their games or activities, (3) spread lies about me, (4) stole something from me, (5) hit or hurt me, (6) made me do things I didn't want to do, (7) shared embarrassing information about me, (8) posted embarrassing things about me online, and (9) threatened me. For school principals' reports, five behaviors are considered to assess school violence: (1) profanity, (2) vandalism, (3) theft, (4) intimidation or verbal abuse among students, and (5) physical injury to other students.

National Characteristics of Korea, Japan, and the U.S.

National characteristics in Korea, Japan, and the U.S. are presented for comparison. Population, primary language, GDP per capita, education expenditure, education system, compulsory education, gross enrollment ratio, curriculum, number of students, and class size were examined. National indicators and school violence will be compared more detail in Chapter 4.

As Table 1.1 shows, three nations have similarities and differences in education and economic aspects. The population size clearly shows the differences in three countries. Comparing to the Korean population, the Japanese population size is two times larger, and the U.S. population is more than six times larger.

Primary languages in Korea is Korean. Korea has been a homogeneous society for a long time, and the immigration population is still smaller than Japan or the U.S. According to a recent report from the Organisation for Economic Co-operation and Development (OECD), an average of 13% of students are immigrants in OECD countries. 0.2% of Korean students are immigrants, whereas 0.6% of Japanese and

Table 1.1 National characteristics in Korea, Japan, and the U.S.

	Korea	Japan	U.S.
Population[a]	50,792,000	127,749,000	322,180,000
Primary language[c]	Korean	Japanese (Portuguese is used in some regions)	English (Spanish used by 13% of the population of age 5 or older)
Immigrant student as %[b]	0.2	0.6	23
GDP per capita[a]	US$34,549	US$37,322	US$55,837
Education expenditure as % of GDP[a]	5.07 (2015 data)	3.59 (2014 data)	4.99 (2014 data)
Education system[c]	Centralized system	Centralized system	Decentralized system
Compulsory education[c]	9 years (6–14)	9 years (6–14)	13 years (5–17)
Gross enrollment ratio (secondary education)[a]	97.59	102.14	97.18
Curriculum[c]	National curriculum	National curriculum	No national curriculum. State education agencies and local school districts develop curriculum
Number of students[a]	6,003,263	13,609,010	50,203,279
Class size[b]	27.4	32.2	25.7

Note Presented data here are in 2015 or latest data
[a]UNESCO Institute of Statistics. Elementary and Secondary level
[b]OECD. Lower secondary level in public school
[c]TIMSS and PIRLS International Study Center

23% of U.S. students are immigrants (OECD, 2019a). Despite the small percentage of immigrant students in Korea, Korea has rapidly changed into a more ethnically diverse society since the 1990s. The Korean local government encouraged marriage migration, which brought brides mostly from the Philippines, Vietnam, and China into the country. This policy had more prevalent effects in rural areas where young Korean women were moving to the cities for better job opportunities, and the men left married foreign women who were willing to stay in the rurality. This policy signif-icantly contributes to the increasing immigrant population in Korea. The number of multicultural families based on the marriage migrant policy was 24,387 as of 2014. As result, the number of bi-ethnic adolescents increased from 9,389 in 2006 to 67,806 in 2014, and those adolescents make up 1.1% of the Korean adolescent population (Chang & Wallace, 2016; Kim et al., 2016; Lee, Lee, & Park, 2016; Statistics Korea, 2014). Language issue in school eventually arose from the rapid growth of a bi-ethnic student population. A national survey showed that about 12% of those students reported school maladjustment because of lack of Korean language proficiency (Ministry of Gender Equality and Family, 2019). In Japan, Japanese is the primary language in schools, yet a small percentage of people use Portuguese, a result of the labor immigrant policies from Brazil during the 1990s in certain areas (Yoshida & Aoki, 2017). According to a national survey by the Minister of Educa-tion, as of 2016, Japanese public schools have 34,335 students who lack Japanese language proficiency, and this is 42.9% of the total of non-Japanese students (Yoshida & Aoki, 2017). In the U.S., English is the primary language, yet 13% of the entire population above the age five use Spanish. As of 2016, about 4.9 million students in public schools (9.6%) were identified as an English language learner (National Center for Education Statistics, n.d.).

Regarding gross domestic product (GDP), Korea has a lower GDP than Japan or the U.S. Korea is at $34,549, when Japan is at $37,322, and the U.S. is at $55,837.

Education expenditure is the highest in Korea (5.07) and it is the lowest in Japan (3.59). The U.S. falls in between (4.99). From primary to tertiary levels of education, Korea's spending on education is higher than the OECD average as of 2019 (OECD, 2019c).

Korea and Japan have a centralized education system, whereas the U.S. has a decentralized education system. Since 2008, the Korean government granted more autonomy to the 17 metropolitan and provincial offices, which focused on school inspection and budgets. However, Ministry of Education still have control over major educational policies, such as the national curriculum and funding systems. More than 75% of school funding is provided by the Minister of Education; private schools (13% out of schools) also receive funding from the Minister of Education. Schools use national curriculums, which are revised every five to 10 years (Center on International Education Benchmarking, 2020). Years of compulsory education are 9 years in Korea and Japan, whereas it is 13 years in the U.S.

Gross enrollment ratio at the secondary education level is 97.56 in Korea, which is slightly higher than the U.S. (97.18) but lower than Japan (102.14). Gross enrollment ratio refers to the percentage of students enrolled in school out of the total number of the entire population at that age. It includes early and late enrollment or repeaters;

thus, the gross enrollment ratio can be greater than 100 (United Nations Educational, Scientific and Cultural Organization 2015).

Korea and Japan have a national curriculum, whereas the U.S. gives each state's education agency and the local school district control over the curriculum. As mentioned above, in Korea, the Ministry of Education has control of the curriculum, yet schools have some degree of autonomy (e.g., adding other content), and certain type of school, such as autonomous schools, have more autonomy than regular schools.

The number of students in Korea is about six million, which is the smallest among the three countries. Japan has more than two times of students (13 million), and the U.S. has about eight times more students (50 million) than Korea.

Regarding the class size (average number of students per class) at the lower secondary school level, Korea is at an average of 27.4, Japan is at 32.2, and the U.S. is at 25.7. Class size is an important factor for effective learning and classroom management. The Korean government initiated reducing class sizes, and it gradually decreased over the past years. At the lower secondary school level, the average class size was 35.7 in 2005, and it has been reduced to below 30 (28.4) in 2016. The average Korean class size at the primary school level dramatically decreased from 32.6 in 2005 to 23.1 in 2017 (OECD, 2019c).

In summary, there are considerable differences in terms of population, number of students, and economic status among the three countries. Korea and Japan share similar education systems and both more homogeneous societies compared to the U.S. Although Korea is economically behind than Japan and the U.S., educational indicators, such as education expenditure and class size, are similar to the other two countries, and Korea has shown improvement over the past years.

Statistics on School Violence in Korea, Japan, and the U.S.

Statistics on school violence have been explored by many researchers and government-initiated surveys. This section briefly addresses statistics on school violence in Korea, Japan, and the U.S., and more detail on this matter will be presented in Chapter 2.

A recent national survey in Korea showed that more than a third of students (35.6%) reported being abused verbally, about 23% of students reported being excluded socially, and about eight percent of students reported experience of cyber-bullying. Elementary school students experience such victimization eight to nine times more than middle or high school students. Serious school violence including physical attack or sexual assault has seen a decrease, yet cyberbullying incidents continues to increase (Ministry of Education, 2019). Another survey data collected from more than 11,000 students in 98 schools in Seoul showed that 41.8% of students experienced school violence in the past year (Yi, 2013). Another study, based on data from 7,000 elementary school students from major large cities, explored how more than 30% of students were involved violence toward their peers, and less than 60%

of offenders felt remorse for their behaviors (Kwon, 2012). From an online survey data of 2,926 students ages 11–16 from randomly selected schools, researchers found more bullies than victims. About 10.2% of students reported being bullied by their peers multiple times in the past term, and 5.8% of students reported victimization (Koo, Kawk, & Smith, 2008). Data of students in Seoul showed that the most common form of bullying is verbal bullying (more than a third) rather than physical (less than 10%) or relational bullying (less than 15%), and bullying incidents tend to decrease among older students (Bae, 2017). As shown, prevalence of school violence in Korea varies by sampling methods (e.g., school level and areas), and the definitions of school violence vary by researchers.

In Japan, youth crime is a more serious concern than adult crime due to an increase over the years (Ohbuchi & Kondo, 2015). Online survey data from more than 6,000 students aged 12–18 revealed that 45% of students were victimized by being insulted, being excluded or being threatened, and 23% of students experienced cyberbullying (Urano, Takizawa, Ohka, Yamasaki, & Shimoyama, 2020). Another survey data collected from 2,334 students in central Japan showed that 36% of students were bullied by a form of bullying, such as being verbally, physically, socially, or sexually and being threatened, and having money or belongings stolen. Verbal bullying is the most common form of victimization and 12% of students reported being an offender while 8% of students reported being both a victim and an offender (Osuka, Nishimura, Wakuta, Takei, & Tsuchiya, 2019).

In the U.S., number of school violence has decreased over the past years, yet many students still face violence at school and become victims to their peers. As of 2016, national survey data showed that 749,400 students aged 12–18 became victims by violent incident at school or on the way to or from school. More serious violent victimization, such as robbery, rape, and sexual assault, occurred 3 students per 1,000 students at school and 5 students per 1,000 students away from school in 2016. About six percent of high school students were victimized by weapon-related violence, and a majority of public schools (69%) had at least one violent incident during the 2015–2016 school year (Musu-Gillette et al., 2018). Over 94% of 59 secondary schools in South Texas reported having bullying incident at least once (Harris & Hathorn, 2006), and data from the California Health Interview Survey (CHIS) Adolescents Data showed that about 16% of students were bullied by peers for the past 12 months and that Black students are more likely to be bullied than other racial groups (Rhee, Lee, & Jung, 2017). More than 2,000 data records from high school students revealed that nearly half of the students (48%) reported being bullied at school (Long & Dowdell, 2018).

Literature has shown bullying as the most common and prevalent at school in the three countries, yet its number of incidents is different within and across countries. This is most likely due to the different measures of school violence incidents depending on the researcher. In addition, time period of recording incidents differs (e.g., weekly, the past last month, six months, or 12 months), and students' education levels and areas could cause variance in frequency of school violence. Thus, it is challenging to compare frequency of school violence from multiple studies with different samplings and measures. This book examines the frequency of school violence focusing on eighth grade students. Analyzing nationally representative samples in Korea, Japan, and the U.S. will be beneficial in the international comparative research. Selecting eighth grade students is also helpful to capture the patterns of school violence as adolescence is when school violence is more frequent than any other age group.

Research Questions

This book seeks to answer five research questions.

(1)   To what extent does school violence occur in Korea? And how do the number and patterns of school violence in Korea differ from those of Japan and the U.S.?

(2)   How do student, parents, teachers, and school principals perceive school violence?

(3)   What do we learn from the comparisons between national characteristics and school violence in Korea, Japan and the U.S.?

(4)   How do school characteristics differ between schools with low- and high-level school violence in Korea compared to those in Japan and the U.S.?

(5)   How do student characteristics and family characteristics link with school violence in Korea, Japan, and the U.S.?

Research question 1 is addressed based on students and school principals' reports in Chapter 2. Student's reports include experience of victimization by peers and by cyberbullies. Principals' reports measured by perceived profanity, vandalism, theft, intimidation, or verbal abuse among students, and physical injury to other students.

Research question 2 is addressed in Chapter 3, and it is based on the literature about various stakeholders' perceptions on students' aggressive behaviors, causes of violent incidents, reactions and strategies against bullying incidents, prevention and intervention strategies, government's policy approaches; perceived school violence and relevant matters including students' perception on school safety, teachers' perception on safety in school and surrounding, teachers' perception on security policies and practices; teacher's perception on student's behaviors, and principals' perception on school violence.

Research question 3 is addressed in Chapter 4, and major international data sources including OECD and WHO were utilized to answer the question. Major types of adult crime in Korea, Japan, and the U.S. are compared, and national indicators under three categories (spending on education, economic status, and violence/delinquency) are presented for each country.

Research question 4 is addressed in Chapter 5. School characteristics include student, parent, and teacher factors and school poverty and location as well. The teacher factor refers to the ability to inspire students and have high expectation on student's academic achievement. The parent factor refers to the support and expectation of students' learning and academic performance and emphasis of high academic standards. The student factor refers to the positive attitudes on school and respect for peers' high achievements.

Finally, research question 5 is addressed in Chapter 6, and major crime theories are briefly explained. For student and family characteristics, student's gender, language minority status, immigration status, academic aspiration and achievement, school attachment, parents' education level, and possession of educational resources at home are included in the analysis.

Research Methods

To address research questions, multiple international datasets, documents, and literature review are utilized. The main dataset for this book is the Trends in International Mathematics and Science Study (TMISS) 2015 survey data. The International Association for the Evaluation of Educational Achievement (IEA) has managed a collection of the TIMSS data since 1995. Every four years, the TIMSS data was collected in multiple countries, and nationally representative samples were selected from each country focusing on fourth and eighth grades. The TIMSS is one of the most comprehensive international survey data that include test scores on mathematics and science achievements, background information about students, teachers, and the schools, as well as perceived students' expectation of their school and learning attitudes. In addition, information about instructional time and resources, perception on academic success, school discipline practices, and school safety were included in the data set from school principals' perspective.

For the TIMSS 2015 survey data, 604,950 students (both fourth and eighth grades), 55,345 teachers, 20,491 principals in 56 countries participated in the survey (International Association for the Evaluation of Educational Achievement, 2017). In this book, data from 20,275 students (5,309 Korean students, 4,745 Japanese students, and 10,221 U.S. students) and 977 mathematics teachers (317 Korean teachers, 231 Japanese teachers, and 429 U.S. teachers) in 543 schools (150 Korean schools, 147 Japanese schools, and 246 U.S. schools) are used and descriptive statistics are conducted to answer research questions. To achieve the research goal of this book, analyzing the TIMSS 2015 survey data has great advantages, and the findings will offer useful insight on school violence phenomenon in Korea, Japan, and the U.S.

Summary

School violence is prevalent around the world. On average, nearly a quarter of students (23%) reported being bullied multiple times a month in the OECD countries (OECD, 2019b, Smith, 2016; World Health Organization, 2020). This book explores school violence phenomenon in Korea from multiple perspectives and from the comparative views from Japan and the U.S. The findings of the book will offer insights for a better understanding of school violence matter and help develop more effective school violence prevention policies.

In this chapter, the definitions of school violence were presented based on the literature, policy documents, and legal documents. School violence is defined differently from different perspectives. Different stakeholders, different culture, and offenders and victims have their own perceptions on school violence. Some researchers view school violence in a broader sense including substance abuse and feeling unsafe at school, whereas others focus on the victim's physical, emotional, and social damage rather than damage done to the victim's possessions. National characteristics in Korea, Japan, and the U.S. were compared as demographic background, education system, and economic status differ by each country. Korea shares more similarities with Japan in terms of being a homogeneous society and its education system. Meanwhile, Korea's economic status is lower than that of Japan and the U.S., yet Korean educational indicators show similarities and further improvement compared to Japan and the U.S.

As addressed earlier, each chapter will present number and patterns of school violence in the three countries. Perceived school violence of various stakeholders, such as students, parents, teachers, and school principals, will be compared among the three countries. National indicators, school characteristics, and student and family factors will be explained along with school violence in each country. Most of the data analysis in this book is based on the TIMSS 2015 survey data, and intensive literature review is also conducted.

References

Akiba, M., Shimizu, K., & Zhuang, Y. (2010). Bullies, victims and teachers in Japanese middle schools. *Comparative Education Review, 54*(3), 369–392.

Bae, S. M. (2017). The influence of strain factors, social control factors, self-control and computer use on adolescent cyber delinquency: Korean National Panel Study. *Children and Youth Service Review, 78,* 74–80.

Bushman, B. J., Calvert, S. L., Dredze, M., Jablonski, N. G., Morrill, C., Romer, D., et al. (2016). Youth violence: What we know and what we need to know. *American Psychologist, 71*(1), 17–39.

Center on International Education Benchmarking. (2020). *South Korea: Governance and accountability.* Retrieved September 14, 2020, from https://ncee.org/

Centers for Disease Control and Prevention. (2020). *Preventing youth violence.* Retrieved September 14, 2020, from https://www.cdc.gov/violenceprevention/youthviolence/fastfact.html

Chang, H., & Wallace, S. P. (2016). Migration process and self-rated health among marriage migrants in South Korea. *Ethnicity & Health, 21*(1), 20–38.

Dussich, J. P. J., & Maekoya, C. (2007). Physical child harm and bullying-related behaviors: A comparative study in Japan, South Africa and the United State. *International Journal of Offender Therapy and Comparative Criminology, 51*(5), 495–509.

Harris, S., & Hathorn, C. (2006). Texas middle school principals' perceptions of bullying on campus. *The National Association of Secondary School Principals Bulletin, 90*(1), 49–69.

International Association for the Evaluation of Educational Achievement. (2017). *TIMSS 2015 user guide for the international database.* Retrieved September 14, 2020, from http://timssandpirls.bc.edu/timss2015/internationaldatabase/downloads/T15_UserGuide.pdf

Ireland, J. L., & Ireland, C. A. (2003). How do offenders define bullying? A study of adult, young and juvenile male offenders. *Legal and Criminology Psychology, 8*(2), 159–173.

Kim, J., Kim, J. Y., & Kim, S. (2016). Super violence, depressive symptoms, and help-seeking Behavior: A gender-stratified analysis of biethnic adolescents in South Korea. *Journal of Preventive medicine & Public Health, 49,* 61–68.

Klein, J. (2012). *The bully society: School shootings and the crisis of bullying in America's schools.* New York University.

Koo, H., Kawk, K., & Smith, P. K. (2008). Victimization in Korean schools: The nature, incidents, and distinctive features of Korean bowling or want-ta. *Journal of School Violence, 4,* 119–139.

Korea Ministry of Government Legislation. (2020). *School violence prevention law (hakgy-opokrekyebangbub, 16441).* Retrieved September 14, 2020, from http://www.law.go.kr/

Kwak, K. & Lee, S. (2016). The Korean research tradition on *wang-ta.* In P. K. Smith, K. Kwak, & Y. Toda. (Eds.), *School bullying in different cultures: Eastern and Western perspectives* (pp. 93–112). Cambridge University press.

Kwon, D. K. (2012). 30% of children used violence against colleagues at school: Survey. *The Korea Times.* Retrieved September 14, 2020, from http://www.koreatimes.co.kr/www/news/spe cial/2012/10/139_122182.html

Lee, C., & Shin, N. (2017). Prevalence of cyberbullying and predictors of cyberbullying perpetration among Korean adolescents. *Computers in Human Behavior, 68,* 352–358.

Lee, J., Lee, R., & Park, M. (2016). Fathers' alcohol use and spousal abuse and mothers' child abuse in multicultural families in South Korea: The mediating role of acculturation and parenting stress. *Children and Youth Services Review, 63,* 28–35.

Long, A. N., & Dowdell, E. B. (2018). Online and health risk behaviors in high school students: An examination of a bullying. *Pediatric Nursing, 44*(5), 223–228.

Ministry of Education. (2019). *Statistics on school violence 2019.* Retrieved September 14, 2020, from https://moe.go.kr/

Ministry of Gender Equality and Family. (2019). *2018 National multicultural family survey.* Retrieved September 14, 2020, from http://www.mogef.go.kr/mp/pcd/mp_pcd_s001d.do?mid= plc503

Musu-Gillette, L., Zhang, A., Wang, K., Zhang, J., Kemp, J., Diliberti, M., & Oudekerk, B. A. (2018). *Indicators of school crime and safety: 2017* (NCES 2018-036/NCJ 251413). National Center for Education Statistics, U.S. Department of Education, and Bureau of Justice Statistics, Office of Justice Programs, U.S. Department of Justice.

National Center for Education Statistics. (n.d.). *English language learners.* Retrieved September 14, 2020, from https://nces.ed.gov/fastfacts/display.asp?id=96

National Center for Injury Prevention and Control. (2016). Understating school violence. Retrieved September 14, 2020, from https://www.cdc.gov/violenceprevention/pdf/School_Vio lence_Fact_Sheet-a.pdf

Ohbuchi, K., & Kondo, H. (2015). Psychological analysis of serious juvenile violence in Japan. *Asian Criminology, 10,* 149–162.

Olweus, D. (2006). *Revised Olweus bully/victim questionnaire (OBVQ)* [Database record]. APA PsycTests. Retrieved September 14, 2020, from https://doi.org/10.1037/t09634-000

Organisation for Economic Co-operation and Development. (2019a). *PISA 2018 results: Combined executive summaries.* Retrieved September 14, 2020, from https://www.oecd.org/pisa/Combined_ Executive_Summaries_PISA_2018.pdf

Organisation for Economic Co-operation and Development. (2019b). *PISA 2018 highlight Indica-tors.* Retrieved September 14, 2020, from https://gpseducation.oecd.org/

Organisation for Economic Co-operation and Development. (2019c). *Education at glance.* Retrieved September 14, 2020, from https://stats.oecd.org/

Osuka, Y., Nishimura, T., Wakuta, M., Takei, N., & Tsuchiya, K. J. (2019). Reliability and validity of the Japan *Ijime* scale and estimated prevalence of bullying among fourth through ninth graders: A large-scale school-based survey. *Psychiatry and Clinical Neuroscience, 73*(9), 551–559.

Rhee, S., Lee, S., & Jung, S. (2017). Ethnic differences in bullying victimization and psychological distress: A test of an ecological model. *Journal of Adolescence, 60,* 155–160.

Smith, P. K. (2016). Bullying: Definition, types, causes, consequences and intervention. *Social and Personality Psychology Compass, 10*(9), 519–532.

Smith, P. K., Kwak, K., & Toda, Y. (Eds.). (2016). Reflections on bullying in eastern and western perspectives. In *School bullying in different cultures: Eastern and Western perspectives* (pp. 399–419). Cambridge University press.

Statistics Korea. (2014). *2014 statistics on the youth.* Retrieved September 14, 2020, from http://kostat.go.kr/portal/eng/pressReleases/1/index.board?bmode=read&aSeq=328722

Sugimoto-Matsuda, J., Hishinuma, E., & Chang, J. (2013). Prevalence of youth violence in the U.S. 1999–2009: Ethnic comparisons and disaggregating Asian Americans and Pacific Islanders. *Maternal and Child Health Journal, 17,* 1802–1816.

Tam, F., & Taki, M. (2007). Pulling among girls in Japan and Hong Kong: An examination of the frustration aggression model. *Educational Research and Evaluation, 13*(4), 373–399.

Urano, Y., Takizawa, R., Ohka, M., Yamasaki, H., & Shimoyama, H. (2020). Cyber bullying victimization and adolescent mental health: The differential moderating effects of intrapersonal and interpersonal emotional competence. *Journal of Adolescence, 80,* 182–191.

United Nations Educational, Scientific and Cultural Organization. (2015). *Gross enrollment ratio.* Retrieved September 14, 2020, from https://en.unesco.org/

United Nations Educational, Scientific and Cultural Organization. (2019). *Behind the numbers: ending school violence and bullying.* Retrieved September 14, 2020, from https://unesdoc.unesco.org/ark:/48223/pf0000366483

U.S. Department of Education. (2020). *School survey on crime and Safety: 2019–20 school year.* Retrieved September 14, 2020, from https://nces.ed.gov/surveys/ssocs/pdf/SSOCS_2020_Questionnaire.pdf

Volk, A. A., Dane, A. V., & Marini, Z. A. (2014). What is bullying? *A Theoretical Redefinition. Development Review, 34*(4), 327–343.

World Health Organization. (2020). *Spotlight on adolescent health and well-being*: *Findings from the 2017/2018.* Retrieved September 14, 2020, from https://apps.who.int/iris/bitstream/handle/10665/332091/9789289055000-eng.pdf

Wrighta, M. F., Yanagidab, T., Aoyamac, I., Dedková, L., Li, Z., Kamble, S., et al. (2017). Differences in attributions for public and private face two face and cyber victimization among adolescents in China, Cyprus, the Czech Republic, India, Japan and the United State. *Journal of Genetic Psychology, 17*(1), 1–14.

Yi, W. (2013). 40% students suffer from school. *The Korea Times.* Retrieved September 14, 2020, from http://koreatimes.co.kr/www/news/nation/2013/01/113_128451.html

Yoshida, R., & Aoki, M. (2017, June 13). *Number of foreign students at public schools who lack Japanese language skills hits record high.* Retrieved September 14, 2020, from https://www.japantimes.co.jp/news/2017/06/13/national/number-foreign-students-public-schools-lack-japanese-language-skills-hits-record-high/#.WutMOIgvyUk

Chapter 2
Frequency and Types of School Violence

Problems of School Violence in Korea

Given the prevalence and severity of school violence, ensuring a safer school environment has been a national agenda in Korea. In 2004, the Korean government-initiated school violence prevention policies by establishing an antischool violence and bullying law for a five-year plan. This policy emphasizes protecting students' rights and raising students as healthy members of society. Not only protecting victim and offering guidance and education to perpetrators, but also supporting intensive research, education, and therapy were suggested as required elements for the policy's success (UNESCO, 2017). Despite such efforts, the policies brought little expected outcomes in reducing school violence. In the meantime, multiple bullying suicide of junior high school students occurred in Daegu, and these incidents triggered the development of harsher policies to prevent school violence. The Korean government considered school violence as a major social evil and established the Comprehensive Measure to Eradicate School Violence (CMESV) in 2012. The CMESV policy was strictly implemented to solve school violence, and students involved in violence are to be reported on official students records and receive severe punishment (Kim & Oh, 2017).

As one of such government efforts, research and statistics on school violence have been actively conducted. Frequency and types of school violence are revealed through national statistics, community survey, and academic research. According to a recent report by Minister of Education (2019), 1.6% of Korean students in 4th through 12th grades reported being victimized. Online survey data from 3,720,000 students showed that victimization decreased by grade increases; about 3.6% of elementary school students, 0.8% of middle school students, and 0.4% of high school students reported victimization (Ministry of Education, 2019). Verbal abuse is the most common form of school violence (35.6%), followed by exclusion (23.2%) and cyberbullying (8.9%). Over the past years, serious violence, such as physical attack, sexual assault, and theft, decreased—a result from the government's active

© Springer Nature Singapore Pte Ltd. 2021
S. Han, *School Violence in South Korea*,
https://doi.org/10.1007/978-981-16-2730-9_2

involvement in violence prevention. However, cyberbullying has seen a constant increase (Ministry of Education, 2019).

Research on school violence in Korea revealed several tendencies. School violence is prevalent across different grades. It is also noticeable that younger students are more likely to be involved in violence. Survey data of 11,714 students from 98 elementary, middle, and high schools in Seoul, 41.8% of students was victimized by bullying, physical attack, or harassment at least once during the past year (Yi, 2013). Such violence is prevalent among younger students as well. More than 30% of elementary school students from selected five large cities reported being involved in committing violence toward their peers. Surprisingly, about 16% of the perpetrators did not consider their behaviors as wrong, and eight percent of the perpetuators even reported being satisfied with the violence (Kwon, 2012). Not only its prevalence, but also the nature and brutality of violence become more problematic with youth violence. Taking money, beating, burning hair, attempting to drown, being lifted with a crane, and left in mid-air for multiple hours are some examples of youth violence incidents. The perpetrators' justification for cruel acts is the victim's rude attitude or disrespect. Such cruel violence among students makes even teachers afraid of intervening incidents (Na, 2012a, February 22).

In some cases, youth's violent behaviors lead to the victim's death. Being victimized often creates suicidal thoughts for victims. Looking at a dataset from 11,714 students in Seoul, approximately 40% of students considered suicide at least once, and five percent of students attempted suicide (Yi, 2013). A significant trigger for the government to become involved in violence prevention was a series of 14 suicides within a span of barely two years in one region. Daegu, the fourth-largest city in Korea, had 14 youth suicides from bullying in less than two years. While this has been a shocking and worrisome for the whole nation (Chu, 2013; Kim, 2011; Koo, 2011; Oh, 2013; Yim, 2011; Yonhap, 2012), experts explain that such tragedies might be linked to Daegu culture. In Daegu, parents have especially higher respect for teachers and are less likely to challenge school authority in comparison with other regions. This might cause a lack of personal relationship between teachers and students, which does not encourage students to speak about their school life or feelings to their teachers in general (Na, 2012b, June 5).

With the widespread use of the Internet and social media in particular, school violence and bullying are not limited to the physical environment. Violence and bullying occur not only on school property, but also outside the school (e.g., victim's home) and virtual space. As a result, victims suffer from harm in person as well as in the virtual space. With the increasing use of online applications, younger children become more easily exposed to a culture of violence. Survey results showed that more than 78% of victims experienced their first school violence incident when they were elementary students. Having their own smart phone allows children to connect to others, making it possible for children to be involved in organized violent behaviors (Park, 2013). On average, youth use Internet about 17 hours per week, and it is more likely to increase over the years (Suicide No. 1 cause of death for S. Korean teens, youths, 2018, April 26). Considering such increasing Internet usage among youth, victimization using Internet tools sees a continuous increase into the future.

School violence is a social problem in Korea as its frequency and severity have increased across all school levels nationwide. Presented in the next section are statistics and empirical research on school violence in Korea, Japan, and the U.S.

Frequency and Types of School Violence in Korea, Japan, and the U.S.

School violence is physical, verbal, or emotional harm to individuals, and it extends from the physical environment into virtual space. In this chapter, school violence is examined with the most common forms, such as physical harm, emotional abuse, and social exclusion both in person and online situation.

In Korea, a report of Ministry of Education shows that school violence decreased since 2012, yet many students are still victimized at school. As of 2017, a national online survey of students from 4th through 12th grade showed that 37,000 students were victimized at school. Elementary students are the most vulnerable group compared to middle and high school students, and approximately 26,400 elementary school students experienced school violence. Verbal abuse is the most common form of school violence (34.1%) followed by exclusion (16.6%), stalking (12.3%), and physical attack (11.7%). Places where victimization occurs vary at school: 28.9% in the classroom, 14.1% in the hallway, and 9.6% on the playground. Perpetrators are usually classmates (44.2%) or peers from the same school and same grade (31.8%). In addition, about 50% of such incidents happens during recess and lunch hour (Ministry of Education, 2017). Another study based on the national samples of 62,276 students from 799 middle and high school students showed that about 3% of students were at least once hospitalized due to physical violence by peers or adults for the past 12 months. About 0.5% (303 students) were hospitalized more than five times in the past 12 months due to physical violence. Among those victims, 27% of boys and 25% of girls smoked a cigarette in the past 30 days, and about 33% of victims consumed alcohol in the past 30 days. In addition, 15% of boys and 18% of girls experienced drugs including inhaling butane gas, sniffing glue, or overdosing on cold medicine (Lee & Lee, 2018).

Internet use is common for students in daily life including learning, socializing, and entertaining purposes. A national report (Statistics Korea, 2014) shows that about 40% of teenagers use the Internet 7–14 hours per week and 18% of teenagers use the Internet 21–35 hours per week. Long hours of Internet use are one of the most significant predictors of cyberbullying (You & Lim, 2016), and it is critical for students to manage their time spent and the purpose of their Internet use properly. National data shows that teenagers use the Internet for entertainment (97%), communication (92%), information (94%), education and learning (57%), and managing a homepage or Web site (45%). Under the circumstance where the Internet is widely used, not only teenagers but also younger children are vulnerable to cyberbullying. About 72% of elementary school students have a smart phone, and it could be a tool for cyberbullying without adequate parental supervision (Statistics Korea, 2014). Such wide use of the Internet and having a personal smart phone contribute to the prevalence of cyberbullying among students. A recent national data from 4000 middle and high school students revealed that 34% of students were involved in cyberbullying as either victim, perpetrator or both, and boys are more likely to perpetrate in cyberbullying than girls (Lee & Shin, 2017). Another empirical study, based on 3,449 students in metropolitan areas including Seoul in Korea, shows that about 43% of students committed cyberbullying by spreading false information and cursed or insulted someone on the Internet and about 21% of students reported victimization by cyberbullying (Kim, Epstein, & Kim, 2017). Researchers also found that committing cyberbullying is positively associated with academic stress, being abused by parents and experience of victimization by their peers (Kim et al., 2017; Lee, Hong, Yoon, Peguero, & Seok, 2018).

Ijime, the word for bullying in Japanese, has been a critical social concern in Japan as bullying causes students physical and emotional harm, school absence, and even suicide (Toda, 2016). The national crime rate is lower compared to other countries (Kobayashi & Farrington, 2020; Liu & Miyazawa, 2018; Dawkins & Gibson, 2018; Ohbuchi & Kondo, 2015), yet the youth crime rate is more than five times higher than that adult crime in the country, and youth crime also shows an increase (Ohbuchi & Kondo, 2015). Online survey data from more than 6,000 adolescents aged 12–18 shows the prevalence of victimization in Japan. About 45% of the participants experienced victimization by multiple types (e.g., repeated experience, such as being insulted, excluded from a peer group, or being threatened in the past), and 23% of participants reported cybervictimization (e.g., being posted information or picture without permission or being teased over the Internet). Such traditional victimization and cybervictimization are more likely to be linked to psychological distress and lack of self-esteem (Urano, Takizawa, Ohka, Yamasaki, & Shimoyama, 2020).

Analyzing survey data from 2,334 students grade 4 through 9 in six schools in central Japan, Osuka, Nishimura, Wakuta, Takei, and Tsuchiya (2019) explored three types of bullying subscales: victimization, perpetration, and witness. In this study, victimization was measured using the categories verbal bullying, physical bullying, racial bullying, sexual bullying, exclusion, being threatened, being robbed of money or having belongings damaged, having lies spread, and cyberbullying. Results show that about 36% of students experienced victimization in one type of bullying at least once every 2–3 months. Among those victims, about eight percent were involved in bullying as both bully and victim. Verbal bullying occurs in about 20% of students, which is the most common type of victimization. About 12% of students reported being the perpetrator in at least one type of bullying. About 33% of students reported witnessing bullying incidents, and about 14% of students reported witnessing verbal bullying and 10% of students witnessed physical bullying (Osuka et al., 2019).

Data from more than 2,900 middle school students in a central region in Japan reveal their bullying experience. About 32% of students experienced victimization, and 31% of students reported committing bullying behavior. It is more likely for more boys than girls, and more 7th graders than eight or 9th graders are to be involved in bullying incidents as the perpetrator. In addition, boys are more likely to be bullied by physical violence, and girls are more likely to bullied by exclusion from groups (Akiba, Shimizu, & Zhuang, 2010).

Data from 100 students from two junior high schools in a mid-sized city in Japan showed 16.5% of students as bullies and 10.4% of students as victims. In addition to bullies and victims, students are involved in bullying in various ways. About 13.9% of students are reinforcers who support bullying using indirect means, 13.0% of students are assistants who help bullies, 16.5% of students are defenders who help or comfort the victim, and just 29.6% of students are outsiders who are not involved in the bullying incident in any way (Hara, 2002).

Survey results of 2,923 students between the ages of 12 and 15 showed prevalence of physical bullying, verbal bullying, and indirect bullying (e.g., ignore or exclude someone). About 30.3% of students reported hitting, kicking, or choking another person in the past six months, about 26.9% of students bullied others by calling them names, 17.4% of students reported starting a fight, and 14.2% of students reported hiding, taking or damaging another's belongings in the same period. Indirect bullying tends to be more common than physical or verbal bullying: 40.7% of students reported ignoring another, and 30.9% of students reported excluding someone from a group. In addition, around 30% of students were victimized by being fought against (30.0%), hit or kicked (32.9%), and called names (29.9%). While 18% of students were verbally threatened, 11.5% of students were teased sexually. About 40% of students and 28% of students experienced being ignored and excluded from a group, respectively (Ando, Asakura, & Simon-Morton, 2005).

Survey results and official records of 809 children between the ages of 6 and 15 from institutional care homes showed that more than 60% of the participants had experience of being abused and living in an unstable family environment. About 28% of children committed delinquent behaviors including theft, assault, running away, or acts of violence at school. Between two groups, having delinquent and non-delinquent behaviors, there are no differences in IQ, yet older children and boys are more likely to commit delinquent behaviors than younger children and girls. (Ohara & Matsuura, 2016).

In the U.S., multiple national survey data show the prevalence and types of school violence in U.S. public schools. Although school violence tends to decrease over the years, there is still an enormous number of students victimized at school, and school violence in the U.S. is serious, ranging from emotional and physical harm, sexual violence, drugs- and weapon-related violence, gang-related problems, and death. Musu-Gillette, Zhang, Wang, Zhang, and Oudekerk (2018) present statistics on school violence based on multiple comprehensive national survey data. Among students ages 12–18, 749,400 students were victimized at school and on the way to or from school in 2016. In addition, 601,300 students had such incidents away from school in the same year. While those numbers indicate non-fatal victimization, serious victimization such as aggravated assault, robbery, rape, and sexual assault occurred among three and five per 1,000 students at school and away from school, respectively, in the same age group in 2016. About six percent of ninth through 12th graders experienced being threatened or injured with a weapon at school in the past 12 months in 2015. School violence is prevalent in U.S. schools, a majority of public schools (69%) had at least one violent incident including a fight or physical attack during the 2015–2016 school year, and 39% of public schools had at least one theft incident of items of more than $10 value being stolen. More serious violence, such as rape, physical attack, or threatening with a weapon occurred in 15% of public schools in the 2015 school year. As the Internet continues to be widely used among students, cyberbullying incidents have become increasingly common as well. About 26% of middle and high schools had cyberbullying incidents, schools with large number of students (e.g., more than 1,000 students) are more likely to have a major cyberbullying problem. Gang presence at school was reported at about 15% of schools in urban areas in 2015, and 22% of ninth through 12th graders reported being offered, given or sold illegal drugs on school premises in 2015. A total of 47 violent deaths including homicide and suicide occurred to students and staff in school in 2015 (Musu-Gillette et al., 2018).

Data from 59 secondary school principals in South Texas reported common bullying behaviors as spreading rumors, teasing, calling others hurtful names, stealing others' belongings, hitting or kicking, threatening, intentionally excluding another from a group, and sexually harassing. Over 94% of schools had at least one problem at school, and lunchtime, restroom breaks, and on the way to school were the places the bullying behaviors most frequently occur (Harris & Hathorn, 2006).

A study based on 2,367 samples from the California Health Interview Survey (CHIS) Adolescents Data in 2011–2012 showed that approximately 16% of students experienced bullying victimization including being threatened to beatings at school over the past 12 months. Black students are more likely to be victims, while Asian students are less likely to be victims (Rhee, Lee, & Jung, 2017). Another study focusing on high school students' victimization and health risk shows that nearly half of high school students (48%) out of 2,077 samples experienced victimization to bullying. Among the students who experienced bullying, more than half of bullies and victims were involved in drugs (55% and 54%) or alcohol use (58% and 55%), and nearly half of bullies had cigarette smoking experience (49%). More than 40% of bullies and victims had experience stealing, and more than 30% of bullies and victims had experience with vandalism. When over 90% of the participants use social media every day, cyberbullying is more likely to be prevalent among high school students. More than 20% of bullies and bully-victims had experience harassing someone online (24% and 23%) and playing pranks online (48% and 53%). In addition, male students tend to bully others more than female students (41% vs. 27%), and male students tend to be more involved in bullying physically than female students (36% vs. 29%) (Long & Dowdell, 2018).

In summary, school violence is common in schools in Korea, Japan, and the U.S., and the types of bullying behaviors are also similar in the three countries. Gender difference in school violence rate and types are observed in the three countries, yet more serious violence, such as drugs- and weapon-related violence and gang problems at school, is more commonly reported in U.S. schools than Korea and Japan.

Data, Measures, and Statistical Methods

To examine frequency and types of school violence in Korea, Japan, and the U.S., the Trends in International Mathematics and Science Study (TMISS) 2015 was analyzed. TIMSS is one of the most comprehensive international education datasets. Although this data aims to assess mainly mathematics and science test scores among elementary and secondary school students, the data also includes student, school and teacher background information, students' perception and expectation of school and teachers, and their learning attitudes. In addition, information about instructional resources, perception on the importance on academic success, and school discipline practices and safety policies was included in the dataset based on school principals' reports.

Data for TIMSS has been collected every four years since 1995 in multiple countries focusing on fourth and eighth grades. For the TIMSS 2015 database, 604,950 students (both fourth and eighth graders), 55,345 teachers, 20,491 principals from 56 countries participated in the survey (International Association for the Evaluation of Educational Achievement, 2017).

For this book, data on Korea, Japan, and the U.S. was selected. A total of 20,275 students (5,309 Korean students, 4,745 Japanese students, and 10,221 U.S. students) and 977 mathematics teachers (317 Korean teachers, 231 Japanese teachers, and 429 U.S. teachers) from 543 schools (150 Korean schools, 147 Japanese schools, and 246 U.S. schools) participated the TIMSS 2015 data collection. As school violence is more prevalent in secondary than elementary schools (Agnew, 2003; Akiba et al., 2010; Musu-Gillette et al., 2018; National Center for Injury Prevention and Control, 2016), data was selected from eighth graders for this book.

In this chapter, school violence was measured from two different stakeholders: frequency of victimization reported by students and frequency of violent incidents reported by school principals.

First, nine items of school violence that were responded to by students are presented with measures as follows. Eighth grade students were asked "During this school year, how often have other students from your school done any of the following things to you including through texting or the Internet?" Nine choices were given: (1) made fun of me or called me names; (2) left me out of their games or activities; (3) spread lies about me; (4) stole something from me; (5) hit or hurt me; (6) made me do things I did not want to do; (7) shared embarrassing information about me; (8) posted embarrassing things about me online; and (9) threatened me. Each item was measured with four scales including at least once a week, once or twice a month, a few times a year and never. To examine the frequency and types of school violence in three nations, descriptive statistics were performed. In addition, mean of those nine items was used as school violence to compare among the three countries.

Second method of measuring school violence is based on principals' report. Principals were asked "To what degree is each of the following a problem among eighth grade students in your school?" Six out of nine choices were to be selected: (1) profanity; (2) vandalism; (3) theft; (4) intimidation or verbal abuse among students;

and (5) physical injury to other students. Items were assessed with four scales including not a problem, minor problem, moderate problem, and serious problem.

Comparison of School Violence in Korea, Japan, and the U.S.

School violence assessed by student experience. A total of nine types of school violence based on students' experience were compared in the three countries. The types include being made fun of by peers, being excluded, being victim of false rumors, having their belongings stolen, being physically hurt, being forced to do things, being victim of embarrassing information made public, having embarrassing content posted about them, and being threatened.

Figure 2.1 shows that nearly half of Korean students and Japanese students experienced being made fun of by their peers and more than half of U.S. students had such experience: 46.7% of Korean students, 48.1% of Japanese students, and 57.4% of U.S. students. Overall, a smaller percentage of Korean students experienced being made fun of by their peers compared to Japanese and U.S. students, yet the percentage of Korean students who experienced being made fun of by their peers almost every week is larger than those in Japan and the U.S.: 16.4% of Korean students reported being made fun of by their peers at least once a week, whereas 15.3% and 11.2% of students in the U.S. and Japan reported such experience, respectively.

Figure 2.2 presents the percentage of students who experienced being left out. In Korea, the 14.0% of students reported being left out from games or activities, when 14.9% of Japanese students and 38.8% of U.S. students reported such experience. More than twice the percentage of students were left out in the U.S than those in Korea and Japan; this could be explained by the effects of different classroom organization

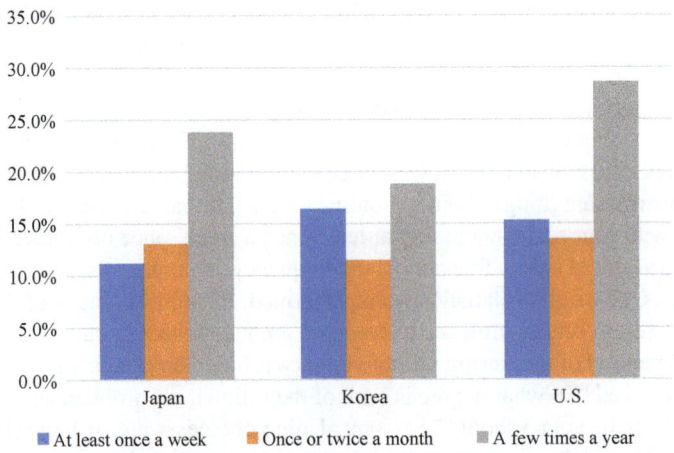

Fig. 2.1 Percentage of students who were made fun of by their peers

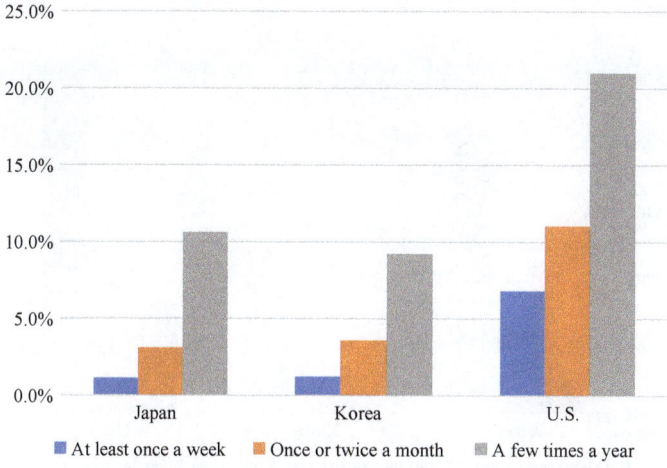

Fig. 2.2 Percentage of students who reported being left out

and teaching styles. Secondary schools in Korea and Japan assign students in a class with a homeroom teacher. Student stays in the same classroom during school hours, and it might help students establish their peer groups. In the case with U.S. secondary schools, students move classrooms for each subject, which leaves students in the classroom without their own peer group. In addition, if classes are implemented with project-oriented instruction or team-based learning, which is more common in the U.S. secondary schools, there are more chances to form a team or group for the classwork. However, in Korea and Japan, a teacher-oriented teaching method is more common, which results in fewer chances to form a team or group in class.

It is also noticeable that being left out is frequent among U.S. students, and 6.8% of U.S. students reported being left out from their peer group every week.

Figure 2.3 shows that fewer Korean students (17.8%) reported having lies spread about themselves compared to Japanese (30.6%) and U.S. students (45.2%). Comparing Korean and Japanese students, U.S. students are more likely to experience such incidents, and about 8.3% of U.S. students were victimized by such incidents at least once a week. Spreading lies is more frequent among U.S. students than their counterparts in Korea and Japan, and its percentage is more than twice that of Korea.

Figure 2.4 shows the percentages of students who reported their belongings stolen at school. Such incident is reported by 11.4% of Korean students, 12.2% of Japanese students, and 32.3% of U.S. students. Less than one percent of Korean students and Japanese students had such an experience at least once a week, whereas approximately five percent of U.S. students had such an experience during the same period. This type of incident occurs to nearly three times more percentage of students in the U.S. than Korea.

Figure 2.5 shows the percentage of students who were physically hurt by others at school. Fewer students in Korea reported physical harm than students in Japan and

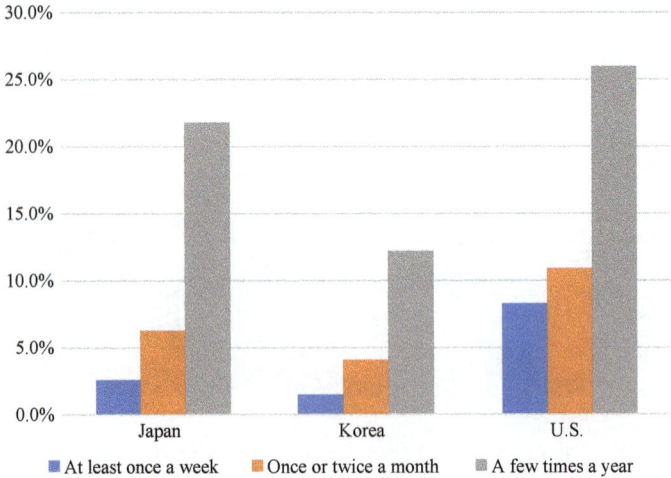

Fig. 2.3 Percentage of students who reported lies being spread about them

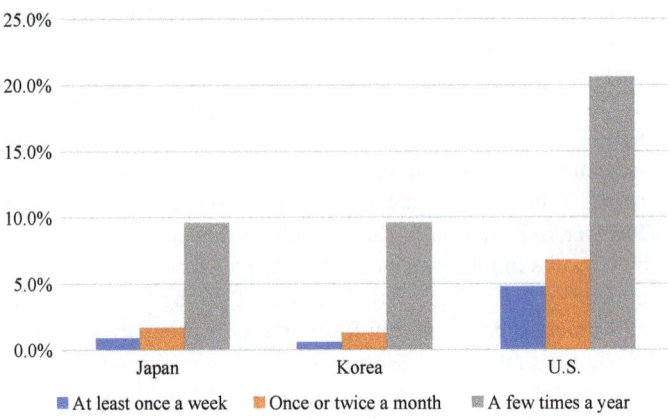

Fig. 2.4 Percentage of students who reported having their belongings stolen

the U.S. (15.3% of Korean students, 19.6% of Japanese students, and 26.9% of U.S. students). This type of incident happened almost every week for 2.6% of Korean students, 3.7% of Japanese students, and 5.7% of U.S. students.

Figure 2.6 presents the percentage of students who were forced to do things. Less than 10% of Korean students (9.5%), more than 15% of U.S. students (16.5%), and about 20% of Japanese students (19.5%) reported such an experience. Being forced to do things by others is more frequent in Japan, and the percentage of students with such incidents are almost double than that of Korea. When we look at this type of incident happening at least once a week, it is about five times more frequent among

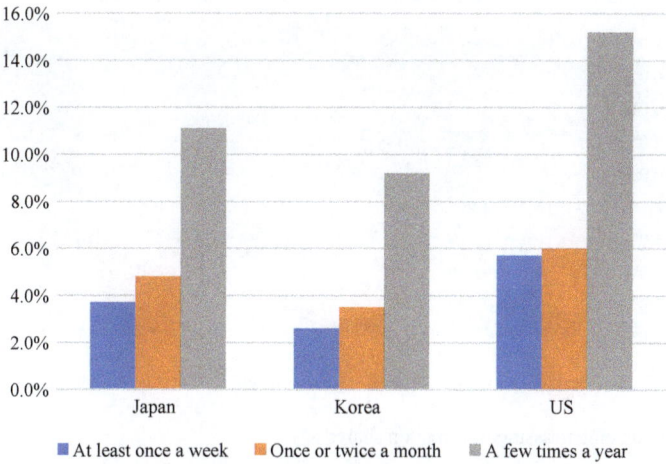

Fig. 2.5 Percentage of students who were physically hurt by others

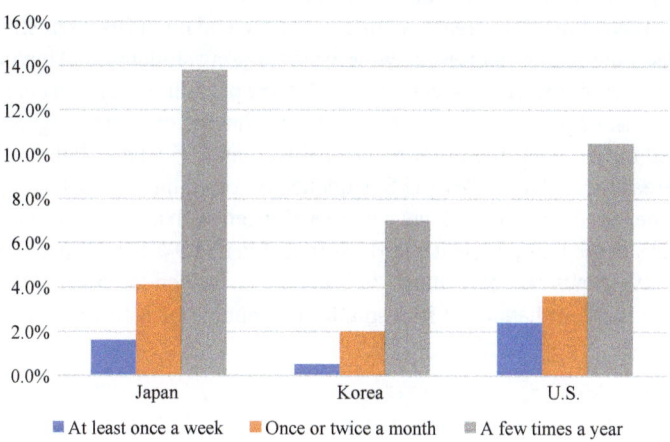

Fig. 2.6 Percentage of students who were forced to do things

U.S. students than Korean students. It happened at least once a week among 0.5% of Korean students and 2.4% of U.S. students, respectively.

As social media and the Internet are widely used by students, any information can be quickly spread to many people. Sharing information could cause social and emotional harm to students, especially when the information degrades an individual's reputation. Such incident among students tends to increase. Figure 2.7 shows the percentage of students who experienced involuntarily having their embarrassing information shared. This type of incident happened to 11.3% of Korean students, 16.8% of Japanese students, and 28.3% of U.S. students. This more commonly

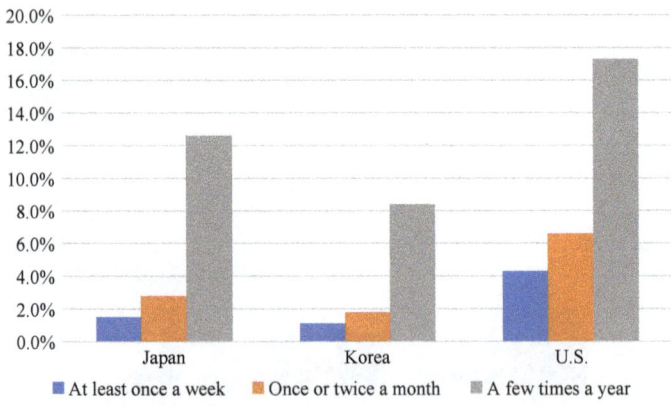

Fig. 2.7 Having embarrassing information shared

occurred in the U.S., and about four times more U.S. students (4.3%) experienced this incident per week than Korean students (1.1%).

Another type of incident regarding Internet and social media use is posting content to embarrass others. Internet is more widely used among students, and having a smart phone dramatically increases socializing with their peers in virtual space. Figure 2.8 shows the percentage of students who experienced having embarrassing things about them posted online. Less than four percent of Korean (3.5%) and Japanese students (3%), whereas more than 13% of U.S. students, reported having such an experience (13.1%). The percentage of students who experienced such an incident at least once a week is 2.2% in the U.S., while it was 0.6% in Korea and 0.4% in Japan, respectively.

Figure 2.9 shows the percentage of students' experiences being threatened at school. This incident happened in a smaller percentage of Korean students (5.3%)

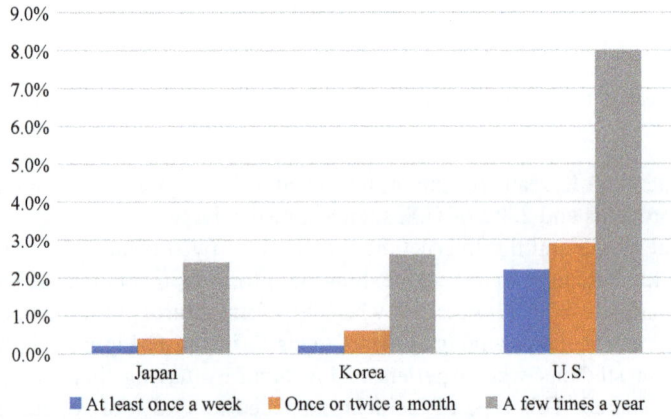

Fig. 2.8 Having embarrassing things posted

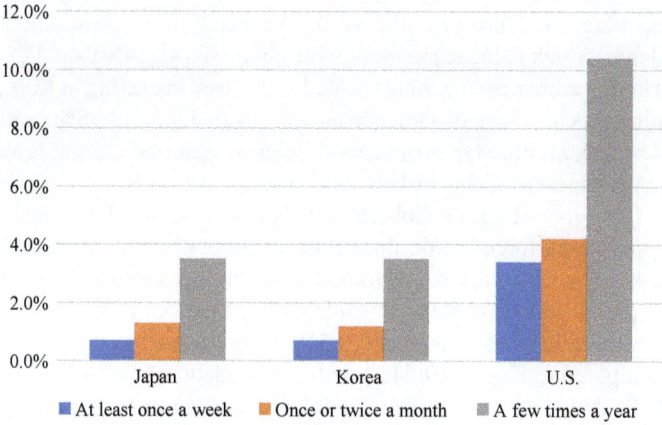

Fig. 2.9 Percentage of students who were being threatened

and Japanese students (5.5%), whereas it happened more commonly among U.S. students (18.1%). Approximately, five times more U.S. students weekly experienced this threat compared to Korean and Japanese students during the same period.

In Fig. 2.10, the percentage of students who experienced each of the nine types of school violence at least once during the past year are presented by country.

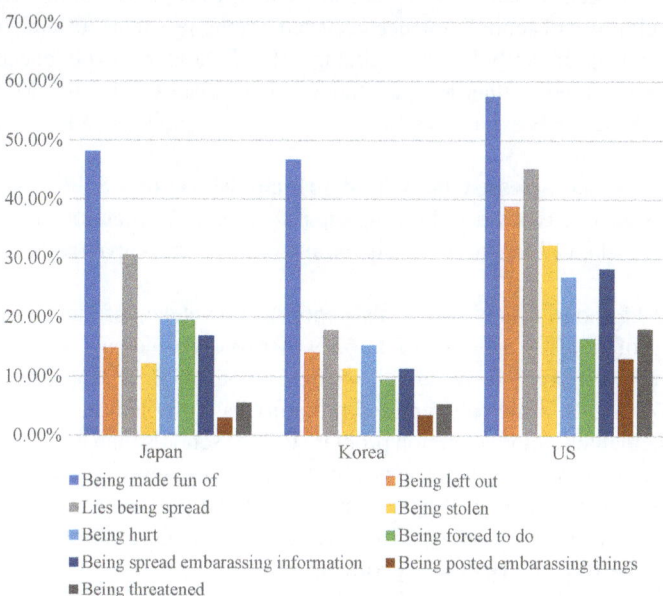

Fig. 2.10 Percentage of student victimization in the past year in Korea, Japan, and the U.S.

In Korea, being made fun of by others is the most common type of school violence among students, which is the same trend with Japanese (48.14%) and U.S. students (57.40%). Having embarrassing things posted is the least occurring in Korea (3.49%) out of all nine types of school violence as well as in Japan (2.98%) and the U.S. (13.06%). Overall, all nine types of school violence occurred among fewer Korean students than Japanese students or U.S. students.

In Japan, four types of school violence (i.e., being made fun of, having lies spread, being hurt, and being forced to do things) occurred in about a quarter of Japanese students. It is noticeable that being forced to do things against their own will is observed as the largest percentage of students in Japan out of the three countries. Nearly one-fifth of Japanese students (19.51%) were forced to do things by others at school, compared to Korean (9.54%) and U.S. students (16.47%).

In the U.S., students experienced school violence more commonly than their counterparts in Korea and Japan. More than half of U.S. students experienced being made fun of by others, and more than 45% of U.S. students experienced having lies spread about them. In addition, more than 18% of students reported being threatened by others, and this is more than three times the percentage of Korean students (5.34%) and Japanese students (5.51%) who had such an experience.

In the three countries, "being made fun of" and "lies being spread" are the most common forms of school violence among eighth grade students, and "having embarrassing things posted" is the least common form of school violence. Overall, incidents measured by nine types of school violence during the past year show the smaller percentage in Korea compared to Japan and the U.S. Except for "being made fun of by others," all types of school violence occurred among less than 20% of students in Korea, while a significantly larger percentage of U.S. students experienced all nine types of school violence than Korean students and Japanese students. More than a quarter of U.S. students experienced six types of school violence at least once in the past year.

School violence assessed by school principals' report. School violence is measured using five types based on principals' reports. As mentioned earlier, 150 Korean principals, 147 Japanese principals, and 246 U.S. principals responded to the questions.

Figure 2.11 shows school principals' report of prevalence of incident involving the use of profanities in school. About 63% of Korean principals reported the use of profanities as a problem in school, whereas about 35% of Japanese principals and about 76% U.S. principals reported profanity as a problem in school. Overall, profanity incident is a more common problem in U.S. schools than their counterparts in Korea and Japan. When we look at profanity incident by severity, different patterns are observed. Most principals in three nations reported profanity occurred, but it is a minor problem: Approximately, 45% of Korean principals, 20% of Japanese principals, and 56% of U.S. principals reported profanity as a minor problem. However, more than 6% of Japanese principals reported profanity is a serious problem, when only 4.7% of Korean principals and 3.7% of U.S. principals reported such incident serious.

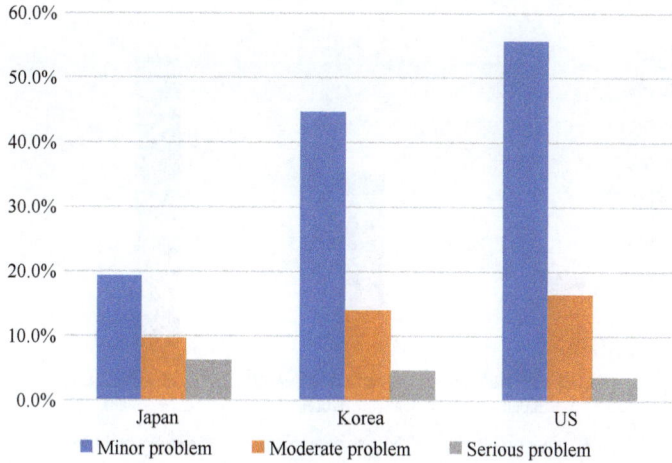

Fig. 2.11 Incidents involving the use of profanities by principals' report in Korea, Japan, and the U.S.

Figure 2.12 shows that more than 41% of Korean principals reported vandalism as a problem, whereas 31% of Japanese principals and more than 42% of U.S. principals reported vandalism as a problem. A similar percentage of Korean and Japanese principals reported vandalism as a serious problem (4.7% and 4.8%, respectively). There are no responses for vandalism as a serious problem among U.S. school principals in the TIMSS survey data.

Figure 2.13 shows that more than 33% of Korean principals reported theft as a problem in school, whereas about 22% of Japanese principals and about 47% of

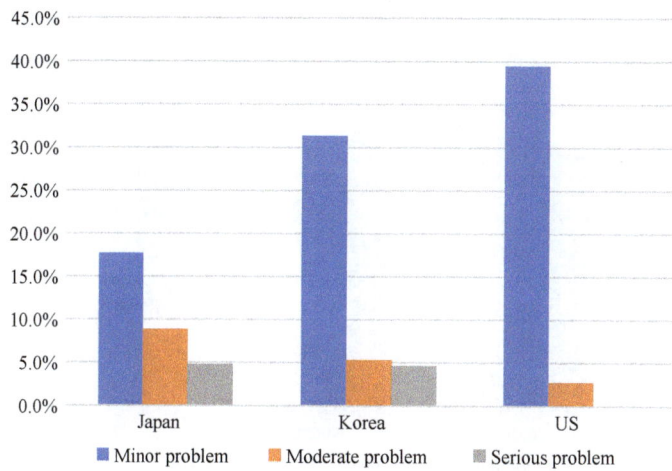

Fig. 2.12 Vandalism incident by principals' report in Korea, Japan, and the U.S.

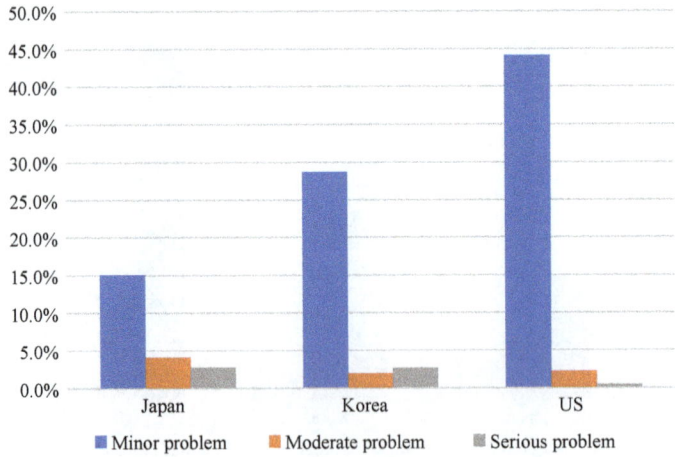

Fig. 2.13 Incidents of theft by principals' report in Korea, Japan, and the U.S.

U.S. principals reported it as a problem. About three percent of principals in Korea and Japan and about 0.5% of U.S. principals reported theft as a serious problem in school.

Figure 2.14 shows that more than half of school principals in Korea, Japan, and the U.S. reported intimidation or incidents involving verbal abuse among students as a problem. While this type of school violence is common across the three countries, fewer Korean schools (64.0%) have intimidation and verbal abuse incidents compared to Japanese schools (70.7%) and U.S. schools (83.6%). In addition, only 2.7% of Korean principals reported intimidation and verbal abuse as a serious problem, yet 8.2% of Japanese principals and 5.5% of U.S. principals reported such

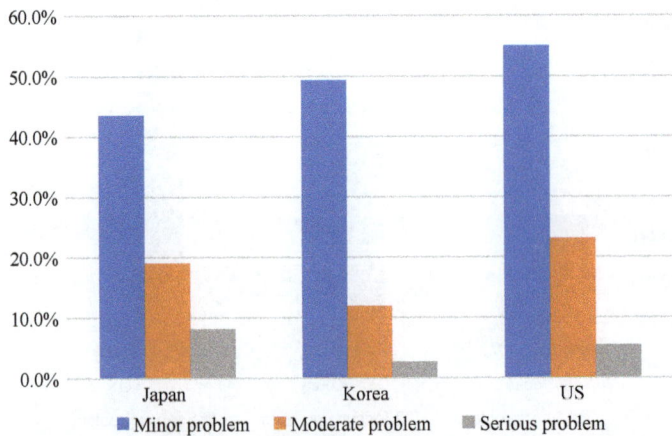

Fig. 2.14 Intimidation or verbal abuse incidents by principals' report in Korea, Japan, and the U.S.

incidents as a serious problem. About two out of ten U.S. secondary schools have intimidation or verbal abuse incident among students.

Figure 2.15 shows that less than half of school principals in the three countries reported physical injury among students as a problem. Approximately, 41% of Korean principals, 39% of Japanese principals, and about 44% of U.S. principals reported that incidents causing physical injury to other students are problematic in school, respectively. On the other hand, physical injury is reported as a serious problem by 3.4% of Japanese principals, 2.7% of Korean principals, and 0.5% of U.S. principals, respectively.

Finally, Fig. 2.16 presents the percentage of schools without a violence problem in the three countries. Each bar presents the percentage of principals who reported each of the five types of school violence as "not a problem" in school. In Korea, 66.7,

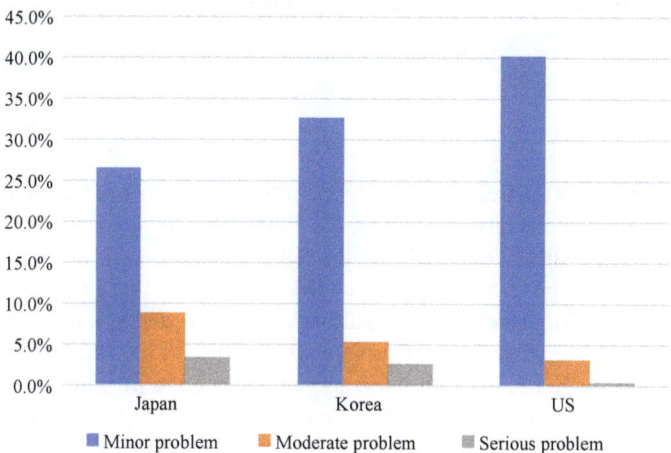

Fig. 2.15 Incidents resulting in physical injury by principals' report in Korea, Japan, and the U.S.

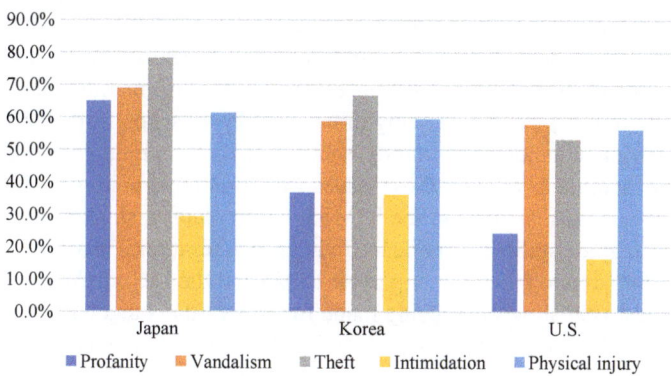

Fig. 2.16 Percentage of schools with no violence problem by principals' report in Korea, Japan, and the U.S.

59.3, and 58.7% of school principals reported theft, physical injury, and vandalism as not a problem in school. In Japan, more than 60% of principals reported theft (78.1%), vandalism (68.7%), profanity (64.8%), and physical injury (61.2%) as not a problem in school. Less than 60% of U.S. school principals reported vandalism (57.8%), physical injury (56.2%), and theft (53.2%) as not a problem in school. As Fig. 2.16 shows, a smaller percentage of school principals in all three nations reported that intimidation and verbal abuse among students are not a problem in school. More schools with no theft problem are observed in Korea and Japan than in the U.S. (66.7% in Korea, 78.1% in Japan, and 53.2% in the U.S.). More schools without a profanity problem are observed in Japan (64.8%), much larger than those of Korea (36.7%) and the U.S. (24.2%). Excluding intimidation and verbal abuse, Japan has more schools with no violence problems overall compared to Korea and the U.S. In addition, the percentage of U.S. schools with no profanity or intimidation and verbal abuse problems are very small, compared to Korea and Japan.

Summary

This chapter presents the frequency and types of school violence in Korea, Japan, and the U.S. based on secondary analysis of the TIMSS survey data. As a quantitative research, there are limitations that are not fully explained on how and why such different or similar patterns of school violence occurs in the three countries. To understand school violence with cultural background in depth, a qualitative study offers unquantifiable information. Despite existing limitations, this study examines school violence in Korea from an international perspective by comparing with the different cultural backgrounds and educational systems of Japan and the U.S.

By analyzing the 2015 TIMSS survey data, the frequency and types of school violence in Korea, Japan, and the U.S. were examined. Two measures by students' experience and school principals' report were used to address school violence. Students reported their experience focusing on nine forms of school violence common in school (Akiba et al., 2010; Harris & Hathorn, 2006; Kim et al., 2017): being made fun of, being left out, having lies spread, having things stolen, physically hurt, forced to do things, having embarrassing information shared, having embarrassing things posted, and being threatened. From school principals' reports, five types of violent incidents (profanity, vandalism, theft, intimidation, and physical injury) were examined, whether those issues were problematic in school or not.

Based on students' reports in the TIMSS survey data, a smaller percentage of Korean eighth grade students experienced violence at least once in school during the past year, compared to their counterparts in Japan and the U.S. students' experience during the past year shows that being made fun of by others and having lies spread about them are the most common forms of violence in all three countries. Having embarrassing things posted is the least frequently occurring in all three countries, yet U.S. students are about four times more likely to experience such an incident than Korean and Japanese students. Being threatened is another form of bullying that occurred the least among students in the three countries, but more than three times of U.S. students experience such an incident than Korean and Japanese students. It is noticeable that the largest percentage of Japanese students' experience being forced to do things at least once, and the largest percentage of U.S. students are victimized at least once in all nine types of violence in school.

Data from school principals' reports reveals that more than 36% of Korean school principals reported no problems with profanity or intimidation, where over 60% of Korean school principals reported vandalism, theft, and physical injury as not problematic. Less Japanese schools had such violence problems than Korea, except for intimidation. The largest percentage of U.S. schools with five types of school violence reported as problems were observed in the three countries.

References

Agnew, R. (2003). An integrated theory of the adolescent peak in offending. *Youth & Society, 34*(3), 263–299.

Akiba, M., Shimizu, K., & Zhuang, Y. (2010). Bullies, victims, and teachers in Japanese middle schools. *Comparative Education Review, 54*(3), 369–392.

Ando, M., Asakura, T., & Simon-Morton, B. (2005). Psychological influences on physical, verbal, and indirect bullying among Japanese early adolescents. *Journal of Early Adolescence, 25*(3), 268–297.

Chu, C. (2013). Teen's death spurs call for action against bullying. *The Korea Herald*. Retrieved September 12, 2020, from http://nwww.koreaherald.com/view.php?ud=20130313000936

Dawkins M., & Gibson C. (2018). *The Juvenile justice system of Japan: An overview*. In J. Liu & S. Miyazawa (Eds.), *Crime and Justice in Contemporary Japan*. Springer Series on Asian Criminology and Criminal Justice Research. Springer.

Hara, H. (2002). Justifications for bullying among Japanese school children. *Asian Journal of Social Psychology, 5,* 197–204.

Harris, S., & Hathorn, C. (2006). Texas middle school principals' perceptions of bullying on campus. *The National Association of Secondary School Principals Bulletin, 90*(1), 49–69.

International Association for the Evaluation of Educational Achievement. (2017). *TIMSS 2015 user guide for the international database*. Retrieved from September 12, 2020, from http://timssandp irls.bc.edu/timss2015/internationaldatabase/downloads/T15_UserGuide.pdf

Kim, E. (2011). Middle school student commits suicide after talking with home room teaching telling her she was a wangtta. *MBC News*. Retrieved September 12, 2020, from http://news.naver.com/main/read.nhn?mode=LPOD&mid=tvh&oid=214&aid=0000199392

Kim, J. E., Epstein, N. B., & Kim, J. (2017). Life stresses in adolescents with problematic media use: The role of anger management in cyberbullying. *Family and Family Therapy, 25*(2), 227–249.

Kim, N., & Oh, I. (2017). Analysis of stakeholders' perceptions of zero tolerance policy for school violence in South Korea. *Journal of Educational Policy, 14*(1), 61–78.

Kobayashi, E., & Farrington, D. (2020). Why do Japanese bully more than Americans? Influence of external locus of control and student attitudes toward bullying. *Educational Science: Theory and Practice, 20*(1), 5–19.

Koo, D. S. (2011). Bullying forces student to take his own life. *The Hankyoreh*. Retrieved March 15, 2017, from http://english.hani.co.kr/arti/english_edition/e_national/511691.html

Kwon, D. K. (2012). 30% of children used violence against colleagues at school: survey. *The Korea Times*. Retrieved September 12, 2020, from http://www.koreatimes.co.kr/www/news/spe cial/2012/10/139_122182.html

Lee, C., & Shin, N. (2017). Prevalence of cyberbullying and predictors of cyberbullying perpetration among Korean adolescent. *Computers in Human Behavior, 68,* 352–358.

Lee, J. M., Hong, J. S., Yoon, J., Peguero, A. A., & Seok, H. J. (2018). Correlates of adolescent cyberbullying in South Korea in multiple contexts: A review of the literature and implications for research and school practice. *Journal of Deviant Behavior, 39*(3), 293–308.

Lee, Y., & Lee, K. (2018). Associations between history of hospitalization for violence victimization and substance use patterns among adolescents: A 2017 Korean national representative survey. *International Journal of Environmental Research and Public Health, 15*(1543), 1–14.

Liu, J., & Miyazawa, S. (2018). Asian criminology and crime and justice in Japan: An introduction. In J. Liu & S. Miyazawa (Eds.), *Crime and justice in contemporary Japan.* Springer Series on Asian Criminology and Criminal Justice Research. Springer.

Long, A. N., & Dowdell, E. B. (2018). Online and health risk behaviors in high school students: An examination of a bullying. *Pediatric Nursing, 44*(5), 223–228.

Ministry of Education. (2017). *The first survey of school violence in 2017.* Retrieved September 12, 2020, from http://moe.go.kr/boardCnts/view.do?boardID=294&boardSeq=71579&lev=0&searchType=null&statusYN=W&page=1&s=moe&m=0503&opType=N

Ministry of Education. (2019). *Statistics on school violence 2019.* Retrieved from https://moe.go.kr/

Musu-Gillette, L., Zhang, A., Wang, K., Zhang, J., Kemp, J., Diliberti, M., & Oudekerk, B. A. (2018). *Indicators of school crime and safety: 2017* (NCES 2018-036/NCJ 251413). National Center for Education Statistics, U.S. Department of Education, and Bureau of Justice Statistics, Office of Justice Programs, U.S. Department of Justice.

Na, J. (2012, February 22). I felt fear of being buried alive. *The Korea Times.* Retrieved September 12, 2020, from http://www.koreatimes.co.kr/www/news/special/2012/07/181_105463.html

Na, J. (2012, June 5). Copycat suicides hit Daegu. *The Korea Times.* Retrieved September 12, 2020, from http://www.koreatimes.co.kr/www/news/nation/2012/06/113_112444.html

National Center for Injury Prevention and Control. (2016). *Understating school violence,* Retrieved September 12, 2020, from https://www.cdc.gov/violenceprevention/pdf/School_Violence_Fact_Sheet-a.pdf

Oh, K. (2013). Seoul to increase security guards, cameras at schools. *The Korea Herald.* Retrieved September 12, 2020, from http://nwww.koreaherald.com/view.php?ud=20130314000717

Ohara, T., & Matsuura, N. (2016). The characteristics of delinquent behavior and predictive factors I Japanese children's homes. *Children and Youth Service Review, 61,* 159–164.

Ohbuchi, K., & Kondo, H. (2015). Psychological analysis of serious juvenile violence in Japan. *Asian Criminology, 10,* 149–162.

Osuka, Y., Nishimura, T., Wakuta, M., Takei, N., & Tsuchiya, K. J. (2019). Reliability and validity of the Japan *Ijime* scale and estimated prevalence of bullying among fourth through ninth graders: A large-scale school-based survey. *Psychiatry and Clinical Neuroscience, 73*(9), 551–559.

Park, S. (2013). 7 cm knife scar photos in my 13 year old daughter's Kakao story. *Nate News.* Retrieved September 12, 2020, from http://m.news.nate.com/view/20130812n02406?f=nate_app&sform=yes

Rhee, S., Lee, S., & Jung, S. (2017). Ethnic differences in bullying victimization and psychological distress: A test of an ecological model. *Journal of Adolescence, 60,* 155–160.

Statistics Korea. (2014). *Youth statistics 2014.* Retrieved September 12, 2020, from http://kostat.go.kr

Suicide No. 1 cause of death for S. Korean teens, youths. (2018, April 26). *The Korea Harold.* Retrieved September 12, 2020, from http://www.koreaherald.com/view.php?ud=20180426000581

Toda, Y. (2016). Bulling (*Ijime*) and related problems in Japan history and research. In P. K. Smith, K. Kwak, & Y. Toda (Eds.), *School bullying in different cultures: Eastern and Western perspectives* (pp. 73–92). Cambridge University press.

UNESCO. (2017). *School violence and bullying Global status report.* Retrieved September 12, 2020, from http://unesdoc.unesco.org/images/0024/002469/246970e.pdf

Urano, Y., Takizawa, R., Ohka, M., Yamasaki, H., & Shimoyama, H. (2020). Cyber bullying victimization and adolescent mental health: The differential moderating effects of intrapersonal and interpersonal emotional competence. *Journal of Adolescence, 80,* 182–191.

Yi, W. (2013). 40% students suffer from school. *The Korea Times.* Retrieved September 12, 2020, from http://koreatimes.co.kr/www/news/nation/2013/01/113_128451.html

Yim, S. (2011). Student bullied over game commits suicide. *Korea Joongang Daily.* Retrieved September 12, 2020, from http://koreajoongangdaily.joins.com/news/article/article.aspx?aid= 2946117

Yonhap. (2012). 2 teenagers get jail term for bullying friend until suicide. *The Korea Times.* Retrieved September 12, 2020, from http://www.koreatimes.co.kr/www/news/nation/2013/08/ 117_105283.html

You, S., & Lim, S. A. (2016). Longitudinal predictors of cyberbullying perpetration: Evidence from Korean middle school students. *Personality and Individual Differences, 89,* 172–176.

Chapter 3
Perception of School Violence from Stakeholders' Perspectives

School violence is a critical issue around the world, and it tends to become more common in schools, increasing victimization for student as well as teachers. A recent study revealed that teacher victimization has seen an increase in Korea, where there is culturally a higher respect for the role of teachers (Moon & McCluskey, 2016), and about 10% of public school teachers in the U.S. experienced being threatened at school by a student during the 2015–2016 school year (Musu-Gillette, Zhang, Wang, Zhang, & Oudekerk, 2019).

While it is agreeable that school violence negatively impacts students' learning environment and teachers' work performance (Smith & Smith, 2006), it does not mean there is the same perception on school violence among different stakeholders. Students, teachers, school administrators, and parents differently perceive the frequency and severity of school violence, reactions toward school violence, and strategies of preventing school violence.

As discussed earlier in this book, school violence is defined at various levels, from making fun of someone to committing physical assault and even murder. With a wide scope of defining school violence, researchers tried to assess school violence in many empirical studies. For example, to measure frequency of school violence, researchers directly assess students' experience of violent incidents. This method might be accurate in case teachers and principals do not reveal all incidents at their school. That is, teachers are more likely to be aware of violent incidents in their own classroom rather than the whole school, and school principals become aware of incidents through discipline practices mostly reported by classroom teachers. When we see school violence reports only through school staff members, minor incidents can easily go unnoticed, and this problem causes underestimation of school violence.

While investigating school violence through students' experience is valuable, exploring the perception of teachers and school administrators is equally important. Perception of school staff members on school violence plays an important role in improving discipline practices and promoting school safety policies. Empirical studies have demonstrated how the perception of school violence among students, parents, teachers, and principals is inconsistent, which challenges implementing

© Springer Nature Singapore Pte Ltd. 2021
S. Han, *School Violence in South Korea*,
https://doi.org/10.1007/978-981-16-2730-9_3

effective school safety policies (Akiba & Han, 2007; Bergmüller, 2013; Demaray, Malecki, Secord, & Lyell, 2013; Harris & Hathorn, 2006; Klein, 2012).

For example, teachers are the ones who most often interact with students than other staff members, and it can be assumed that teachers notice happenings among students. This assumption was addressed in the previous studies, and researchers emphasize that teachers can help minimizing violence in school by intervening bullying incident and by fostering school belonging (Mucherah, Finch, White, & Thomas, 2018; Norwalk, Hamm, Farmer, & Barnes, 2015). More importantly, students perceive that teachers' intervening is most helpful to stop bullying incidents (Crothers, Kolbert, & Barker, 2006; Kearney & Smith, 2018) and building a positive relationship between teachers and students is a protective factor against bullying (Longobardi, Lotti, Jungert, & Settanni, 2018).

In addition, principal's perception of school safety and their role in it has a critical influence in preventing school violence and maintaining an orderly learning environment (Harris & Hathorn, 2006; Kearney & Smith, 2018). Equally importantly, parents' awareness of victimization at school is essential for preventing violence because they protect and support children at home and the neighborhood (Sawyer, Mishna, Pepler, & Wiener, 2011). Not only physical victimization but feeling fear at school also should be measured for ensuring a safe school because students' fear at school tends to negatively impact their school performance and attendance (Akiba, 2010).

Altogether, it is worthy examining the perception of parents, students, teachers, and principals on school violence because their perspectives are critical in preventing student victimization. Studies showed that little consensus on school violence among stakeholders might become a barrier for fostering safer schools (Benbenishty & Astor, 2005; Demaray et al., 2013).

In this chapter, various stakeholders' perceptions on school violence in Korea, Japan, and the U.S. were presented based on the previous studies. Previous studies were selected that were published since 2000 in this chapter. Studies presented here were chosen for their different angles of exploration on stakeholders' perceptions of school violence in each country. It might make more sense if the chosen studies have the same indicators across countries for comparison purposes, yet it is still insightful to see the different indicators in examining school violence issues at each country.

In this chapter, studies on a stakeholder's perception of school violence are addressed as follows. In Korean studies, parents' and communities' perception regarding the level and cause of school violence, students' and mothers' reactions to and perceptions of aggressive behaviors, Korean government's reactions to and policies preventing school violence, teachers' perception on school violence by gender and teaching experience, and comparison of teachers' and students' perception of school violence are presented. In Japanese studies, students' perception of and their justification strategies of bullying behavior, students' forms of bullying behaviors, and student's perceived causes of bullying incident are presented. In U.S. studies, principals' perceived school safety, bullying incidents and discipline practices, teachers' perceived effective bullying practices, students' feeling of fear at

school, students' perception of effective bullying prevention strategies and students
and their mothers' reasons for not committing aggressive behaviors are presented.

Stakeholders' Perspectives on School Violence in Korea

A survey result based on a dataset of 927 shows that about 82% of the participants perceive school violence as a serious problem. More than 60% of the participants become aware of school violence through mass media, and only 1.08%
of the participants are informed through the school. In addition, the participants
perceive that social environment (44.9%), home environment (29.1%), and school
environment (10.1%) are responsible for causing school violence. The participants
perceive that prevalent social cultural factors (40.2%) and insufficient parental factors
(31.8%) contribute to occurrence of school violence, and only 6.5% of participants
perceive school counseling as responsibility for occurring school violence (Korean
Educational Development Institute, 2005).

A teacher's role is important in preventing school violence, and a study explored
ignorance vs. taking action as teachers' responses to bullying scenarios. The study,
based on an online survey of 146 Korean teachers, found that female teachers are
more likely to take action and teachers with more than 26 years of work experience
are less likely to take action. In addition, there are no difference between teachers'
reactions regardless of if they had antibullying training or have antibullying policies
in school (Yoon, Bauman, Choi, & Hutchinson, 2011).

Another survey result shows the perception of school violence among teachers
and students in Korea. Survey data based on 424 students and 136 teachers from
seven different middle schools in Seoul revealed that nearly half of the students were
victimized at least once, and more than 30% of teachers and students reported school
violence incidents as occurring 1–2 times a month (35.2% and 32.9%, respectively).
Male students are more likely to be victimized, and about seven percent of male
students experienced victimization over 13–15 times. About 57% of teachers and
41% of students perceived school violence are very or rather serious out of a scale of
five. About 44% of teachers and students believe the offender commits violence with
no reason and 23% of teachers and 20% of students indicate the offender commits
violence to steal money. In addition, teachers and students perceive that the offenders
are usually their classmates, rather than seniors or students from other schools (74.1%
and 68.3%, respectively). While teachers and students perceive that the offenders are
continuously involved in violence without contemplation or regret (38.1% and 48%,
respectively), teachers and students perceive that victims are less likely to ask for help
in of fear of reprisal by the offenders (70.5% and 56.9%, respectively). Perception
about school violence between teachers and students as presented above is shared in
a quite similar way, yet several distinct perception gaps were observed. For example,
more teachers tend to perceive school violence as a serious problem than students
do (57.2% vs. 41.1%), teachers pointed out home (67.4%), and school (17.4%)
as causes for school violence, whereas students pointed out school (48.6%) and

home (15.8%). In addition, teachers perceived negative home environment including students' family background (e.g., parent divorce or remarriage) as serious reasons for school violence, whereas students pointed out negative influence of peer, culture, and social media as cause of school violence (Kwon & Kim, 2015).

According to the survey data results based on more than 64,000 teenagers in Korea, teenagers who do not live with parents (e.g., live with relatives or friends or live in facilities or dormitories) are more likely to become victims of violence than their counterparts living with parents. In addition, teenagers who have a father or mother of foreign origin are more likely to become victims of violence (Park, Lee, Jang, & Jo, 2017). Another national survey result shows that there are various perceived reasons for being victimized. Students were asked why they were victimized and more than half of victims responded for no specific reason for being victims, while about 12% of victims perceived their personality as a problem. Less than 10% of victims responded their small body size or physical weakness or blamed their own behaviors (Statistics Korea, 2014).

Students' age shows different perceptions about aggressive behaviors. A study based on 113 students and adults (workplace personnel and mothers) in Korea showed how the participants perceive physical and verbal aggression incidents. The participants were asked to see cartoons about aggression and to report their responses. Older students (15 to 17 years old) and mothers tend to accept less aggressive behaviors, whereas younger students (10 to 15 years old) and workplace employees tend to justify aggressive behaviors by pointing out victims' responsibility (Lee, Smith, & Monks, 2011).

While the Korean government emphasized antibullying policies, the government also initiated intensive research about school violence prevention. Such research helps develop more effective school violence prevention. For example, case studies suggested that school violence prevention should be established at the individual school level, and students, teachers, and principals should build a closer relationship with one another. In addition, schools should foster students' feeling safe at school by creating sound classroom and school culture. Teachers should make an effort for improving students' well-being as well as academic achievement (Park et al., 2014).

In summary, while school violence prevention is required of all stakeholders' active involvement, particularly the teachers' role is stressed in intervening violence. Teachers' reactions to school violence incidents differ by gender and teaching experience year. The channel of getting information of school violence differs by stakeholders, and perception of cause of school violence is also inconsistent across different stakeholders. Perception on aggressive behaviors is inconsistent by different age groups among the same stakeholders. The government is aware of school violence prevention as a national agenda and enforces strict legal standards while supporting intensive research for exploring school violence status and effective prevention policies. Educational researchers share their suggestions on reducing school violence with changing the school culture, improving school bonding among students and school staff and stressing involvement of parent and community.

Stakeholders' Perspectives on School Violence in Japan

Japan has been known as one of the safest countries in terms of having a lower rate of crime, yet school violence is still a main concern in Japanese society. Not only the frequency of youth crime, but also its continued increase is a critical social problem (Ohbuchi & Kondo, 2015). According to the Programme for International Student Assessment (PISA) report, bullying is a prevalent problem in Japanese school, and certain forms of bullying occur more commonly than their counterparts in the Organisation for Economic Co-operation and Development (OECD) countries. For example, Japanese students are more likely to be made fun of by others than their counterparts (17% in Japan vs. 11% in OECD average) and more likely to get hit or pushed by others than their counterparts (9% of in Japan vs. 4% in OECD average) (OECD, 2017). Some Japanese schools take precautions in not only bullying incidents among students, but also unexpected serious crimes including injuries and death caused by mentally ill intruders. Those Japanese school officials adopt security camera systems and provide self-defense courses as well as tear gas canisters to teachers (Sims, 2001).

Bullying has gained public attention in 1984 and 1985 in Japan when 16 suicides were revealed bullying-relevant incidents (Srabstein & Merrick, 2013). Since then, school violence incidents in Japan have rapidly increased, and as of 2016, more than 320,000 bullying incidents were reported. Bullying incidents increased 1.5 times more at the elementary school level compared to the past year, and experts explained that environmental factors might be a main cause of bullying incidents, including cyberbullying using the Internet ("Reports of school bullying," 2017). In addition, having more support from adults and frequent interactions with different age groups would help students to reduce bullying incidents ("Report of school bullying," 2013). While various bullying prevention efforts have been made from the government to local communities, deeply rooted collectivist culture and a highly valued aspect of harmony in Japanese society make such efforts more challenging. Bullying happens in Japanese schools as a larger group rather than a couple of individuals, and it makes it harder for victims and bystanders to avoid or intervene incidents ("Why bullying in Japanese schools", 2017). It is considered that bullying victims are inferior or weak people in Japanese tradition, yet someone who does not stay in line of group harmony or shows positive attributes such as outstanding performance also can become a target of bullying (e.g., high achievers as well as low achievers) (Srabstein & Merrick, 2013).

Some researchers have attempted to explore students' perception on bullying focusing on cultural factors. According to empirical studies, Japanese students' perception about justification on bullying behaviors might be related to group-oriented culture. Hara's (2002) study, based on the data from 100 students in two junior high schools in Japan, showed justification strategies for bullying behavior. Survey results showed that students have various bullying justification strategies. For instance, some students deny responsibility for their behavior and instead blame their family background or bad peers. Others ignore their behavior for damaging victim's possession and/or hurting feeling and sometimes blame the victim's behaviors. Data showed that about 16.5% of students bullied their peers and a majority of students (more than 86%) consider bullying as right or acceptable behavior. This prevalent perception appears among students regardless of their roles as either bully, victim, defender, reinforcer, assistant, or outsider. In addition, 100% of bullies and even 62.5% of victims blame the victim's behaviors. While such perception on bullying behavior widespread, different justification strategies were found between male and female students. Male students are more likely to blame the victim's behavior or personality (80.0% vs. 71.7%), whereas female students than male students are less likely to concern victim's injury or damage (13.2% vs. 6.7%) (Hara, 2002).

Another study based on the data from junior high school students in Japan and England showed that Japanese students are more likely to act as a larger group. The study revealed that Japanese students are more likely to bully a victim as a larger group, even including the victims' friends, whereas English students are more likely to attack a victim as a small group of bullies, most bullies also being older students. Students both in Japan and England are less likely to seek help from others because of fear of retaliation, having no one they trust or a lack of confidence (Kanetsuna & Smith, 2002). The finding is consistent with Hara's (2002) study that Japanese bullies tend to act as a large group and choose their peers as victims rather than younger students. Another comparative study in Japan and the U.S. based on a dataset of 584 Japanese college students and 623 U.S. college students shows that Japanese students had more experience with bullying behavior when they were in high school. In addition, Japanese students tended to believe bullying behavior (e.g., intentionally and repeatedly harming another person physically or mentally) is not wrong unlike U.S. students (Kobayashi & Farrington, 2020).

While school violence has often been compared among populations with distinct cultures, such as western and eastern countries, some studies showed differences in school violence within countries of similar eastern cultures. A study has shown factors associated with deviant behaviors in Japan and Taiwan. Data of 516 Taiwanese students and 476 Japanese students in 5th or 6th grade was analyzed to reveal what factors affect students' deviant behaviors. In this study, deviant behaviors were measured based on students' self-reports on their behaviors. For example, how often they talk back to teachers, use abusive language, express opposite views against teachers, or comply with teachers' requirements. Data analysis revealed that more students involved in deviant behaviors in Japan than their counterparts in Taiwan. About half of Japanese students agreed to the statement "frequently use abusive language," yet less than 30% of Taiwanese students agreed to the same statement. In addition, Japanese students' behaviors are more likely to be impacted by social control, while Taiwanese students' deviant behaviors are more likely to be impacted by authoritative teacher's discipline. That is, Japanese students are less likely to commit deviant behaviors if they are afraid of being punished by the teachers, getting legal sanctions, being judged by others or being disliked by peers. On the other hand, Taiwanese students are more likely to commit deviant behaviors if they perceive their teachers scold harshly and loudly, require obedience of rules without exceptions, or treat students unfairly (Chen, Cheng, Liang, & Sato, 2012).

In summary, empirical studies reveal that school violence is influenced by unique Japanese culture. Types of school violence might be formed based on group-oriented culture, like a number of students designating and bullying a single victim who does not belong to the majority group (an individual who is either exceeding or lacking than the average performance and/or other attributes). In Japan, a main defense for bullies is rationalization of their bullying behaviors in their culture; victims are indicated as those who do not contribute to group harmony, which is highly valued in Japanese society.

Stakeholders' Perspectives on School Violence in the U.S.

Empirical studies on school violence have been well established in the U.S., compared to Korea and Japan. In addition to the considerable number of studies, various approaches have been applied to explore school violence in the U.S. One of the contributions for dynamic research in school violence might be an ethnically diverse population and a broader range of cultural background among students. Summarized research results on school violence are below, and those studies are conducted at national, state, district, and school levels as well as secondary national data, survey results, and/or interviews with individual stakeholders.

Nationally representative data shows that more than five percent of U.S. students ages 12–18 reported fear of being attacked or harmed. Some students felt such fear at school (3.3%), and others felt this fear away from school (2.2%). Such perceived fear is observed differently by gender and school location. Female students were more likely to feel fear than male students, and about 6.2% of 6th grade students and 4.7% of students in urban areas were afraid of being attacked or harmed in school and avoid certain school settings (Musu-Gillette, Zhang, Wang, Zhang, & Oudekerk, 2017). Another study showed that about 9.9% of fifteen years old students often feel fear of potentially being attacked or harmed at school (Akiba, 2010). Although these studies show no report on an actual violent incident, knowing students' fear at school is an important indicator assessing school safety. Such fear might be developed by witnessing or hearing about incidents, and it should be taken seriously by school staff members.

Some studies explore students' perception on effective bullying prevention. A survey study in Pennsylvania revealed students' preference of antibullying strategies. A total of 285 middle school students were asked to respond on the effectiveness of different antibullying strategies. Students reported teachers and parent involvement as most helpful. That is, students believe that recruiting the teachers helps in stopping bullying as well as notifying both parents of the victims and bullies about bullying incidents as most effective (Crothers et al., 2006). It is especially important as most parents take actions for their child's victimization, and it is critical to prevent future bullying problems. A study explored parents' responses to their child' victimization. More than 1,100 parents who have a victimized child responded to ten possible options regarding their child's victimization, and a majority of parents

(86.5%) indicated talking to their child. Parents also indicated speaking with a school administrator or counselor (30%, respectively), the child's teacher (19.0%), separating the child from the other student (16.3%), and speaking with the other student's parent (9.2%). Some parents let their child fight back (5.9%), while less than five percent of parents indicated talking directly to the other students involved in the bullying incident, as well as ignoring the incident or doing nothing, and taking legal actions (Johnson, Waasdorp, Gaias, & Bradshaw, 2019). This clearly reconfirmed that bullying incidents could be solved by trusted adults, teachers, and parents. Such perception is supported by another empirical study.

A study showed that when teachers support stopping bullying and protecting students from bullying, those schools are more likely to reduce bullying incidents. Data of 1,554 teachers and 198 school principals collected from 104 Texas elementary schools reveals that teachers' protection and principals' understanding of their role have potential benefits in reducing bullying incidents (Kearney & Smith, 2018). Despite students' perception and empirically proven strategies on reducing victimization at school, teachers are less likely to be aware of such victimization than students. Demaray et al. (2013), based on 137 students and six teachers in a private school, found more frequent victimization among 3rd and 4th graders than older students, yet no gender difference in prevalence of victimization. A significant gap on the level of bullying incidents was observed. Overall, there is little agreement on frequency of victimization between students and teachers, students reported the highest level of bullying victimization, whereas teachers reported the lowest level (Demaray et al., 2013).

Often, researchers utilize principals' perceived school violence as actual level of school violence. A study revealed principals' perception about bullying by conducting a survey with 59 junior high and middle schools in Texas. The results showed that more than half of principals reporting that they sometimes or often noticed bullying incidents (e.g., hit or kick, stealing, name calling, teasing, and spreading rumor). Principals' perception on school violence showed difference by principals' gender and years of work experience. That is, female principals tend to be aware of things stolen than male principals, and principals who have 4 to 10 years of work experience tend to be aware of students intentionally being left out than principals with less than 4 or more than 10 years of work experience. Participating principals perceived their schools to be safe based on response of faculty members' commitment on stopping bullying when it happens (i.e., 4.2 through 4.9 out of 1 through 5 scale). While principals perceive their schools as safe, they agree that staff training, class discussion about bullying, monitoring by staff, community response, and immediate punishment are needed to decrease bullying incidents.

Another study revealed principals' perspectives on disciplinary actions to perpetrators and level of awareness of bullying incidents. Researchers found that such perception also differs by principals' age and ethnic minority status. Older principals (46 years or older) tend to agree that bullies should be punished immediately than younger principals do and ethnic minority principals tend to be aware of bullying incidents in the classroom and the initiation of clubs and teams than White principals do (Harris & Hathorn, 2006). Principals' and teachers' perceptions on discipline practices and bullying incidents are critical because their perception directly impacts disciplinary actions.

Klein (2012) asserted that adults' preconceptions could lead to unfair disciplinary decision. Based on her content analysis of shooting incident documents and interview results with students, she claims that if adults perceive well-educated students from affluent families are less likely to be involved in violent behaviors, then such perception could lead to wrong judgments toward incidents. She also pointed out that there are gaps of perception on school violence between the public and school personnel. The public and school personnel might not share the view of how they take school violence issues seriously as top priorities (Klein, 2012).

While emphasizing a teacher's role, examining teachers' perception is critical in preventing bullying incidents. A study shows teachers' perception on bullying incidents and prevention strategies based on survey results from 359 elementary school teachers. The results show that about 29% of teachers reported having no thought about setting bullying prevention rules, yet more than 86% of teachers were involved speaking with victimized students and bullies for bullying incidents. That is, teachers tend to react once bullying occurs rather than making preventive efforts. In addition, more than 36% of teachers reported having a regular time for bullying prevention activities as time consuming, and more than 33% of the teachers reported that bullying is not a problem in the classroom or less serious of a problem compared to other school issues. Teachers are more likely to have discussion about bullying in the classroom if they have perceived a higher level of bullying. In addition, teachers are more likely to have bullying prevention activities in the classroom if they attended bullying or violence prevention training programs. Teachers perceived post-bullying activities (e.g., contacting parents of the bullies and meeting with bullies, victims, and parents) and improving supervision as the most effective ways to reduce bullying, whereas having a conference day, bullying prevention committee or providing bullying prevention efforts to parents in parent–teacher meetings as least effective (Dake, Price, Telljohann, & Funk, 2003).

It is important to understand how students perceive and control their problem behaviors and how parents control their child's behavior. Some comparative studies reveal how students perceive and control their behaviors differently. Bear and colleagues (2006) collected data from interviews and survey data based on 132 students across five different schools in U.S. and 75 students across three schools in Japan. The findings reveal that U.S. students tend to focus on punishment, rules, overt retribution, and relational retribution, whereas Japanese students tend to be aware of others' physical or psychological needs and consequences caused by their behavior. About 92% of U.S. students responded to punishment as a reason for not committing aggressive behaviors, whereas about 90% of Japanese students did not point out punishment as a reason for not involving aggressive behaviors. That is, U.S. students are more likely to consider the consequence caused by their behaviors, whereas Japanese students are more likely to be concerned for the needs of others. The researchers pointed out that such differences of moral reasoning in Japan and the U.S. are challenging to explain merely by cultural factors (e.g., individualism vs. collectivism), which is not proved by empirical evidence. In addition, as the researchers reviewed previous studies on different emphasis on parenting, students' moral reasoning could be influenced by their parents. That is, U.S. mothers emphasize authority and direct control, whereas Japanese mothers stress more psychological and indirect control toward their child's problem behaviors (Bear, Manning, & Shiomi, 2006). Another comparative study in Japan and the U.S. show how cultural context is related to perception of bullying. It is often assumed that students in group-oriented culture value social acceptance and affiliation more, yet such cultural factors may impact students' perception differently. Data from 449 Japanese middle school students and 189 U.S. middle school students revealed that Japanese students are less likely to fear social rejection than U.S. students and Japanese students are less likely to need affiliation than U.S. students do. Researchers interpret that Japanese students are already adjusted to a collectivist culture and they perceive fewer chances of being rejected, whereas U.S. students, who are familiar to individual-oriented culture, are more likely to fear social rejection and losing affiliation (Lerner, 2011).

In summary, school violence in the U.S. is assessed by various manners including students' fear at school, teachers' perception on effective bullying prevention strategies, principals' perceived level of school violence and discipline practices, and parents' emphasis on reasoning aggressive behaviors. As expected, empirical studies show that there are inconsistencies in the perception of school violence, bullying, aggressive behaviors across students, parents, teachers, and principals. In addition, researchers attempt to explore school violence within cultural impacts and show how stakeholders perceive and react to school violence differently.

Based on the literature review in Korea, Japan, and the U.S., it is assumed that such inconsistencies of perceived school violence issues exist among various stakeholders. The next section presents how school violence is viewed through the same stakeholder's perception in three countries.

Comparison of Perceived School Violence in Korea, Japan, and the U.S.

Data and Analysis

The Trends in International Mathematics and Science Study (TIMSS) 2015 is a main dataset for this book's examination of school violence. As nationally representative data, TIMSS survey data has been internationally collected by the U.S. Department of Education since 1995, and TIMSS 2015 contains data from students, teachers, and schools in more than 50 different countries. Analyzing TIMSS data gives great strength and benefit in comparing educational outcomes and relevant issues across nations.

TIMSS survey data provides data of 4th graders and 8th graders. In this section, data of 8th graders was analyzed because school violence is more common in secondary schools than elementary schools (Agnew, 2003; Akiba, 2010; Musu-Gillette et al., 2017; National Center for Injury Prevention and Control, 2016). The TIMSS survey data is based on 5,309 Korean students, 4,745 Japanese students, and 10,221 U.S. students; 317 Korean teachers, 231 Japanese teachers, and 429 U.S. teachers; and principals from 150 Korean schools, 147 Japanese schools, and 246 U.S. schools.

As school violence is defined broadly, the presented figures below include a variety of measures of school violence and safety issues. A total of six figures present students' perceived safety at school, teachers' perceived safety in school neighborhood, teachers' perceived safety at school, teachers' perception on security policies and practices, teacher's perception on student's behaviors, and principals' perceived school violence.

Students were asked "What do you think about your school? Tell how much you agree with these statements". Students responded to a question "I feel safe when I am at school" with four scales: agree a lot, agree a little, disagree a little, and disagree a lot.

The result in Fig. 3.1 shows that most students feel safe at school in three countries. When we look at the percentage of all students who agree with the statement, about 80% of students in three countries feel safe in school. Approximately, 20% of Korean students agree a lot with having a safe school, whereas more than 28% of Japanese students and 42% of U.S. students agree a lot with the statement. The percentages of students who disagree a lot with the statement were observed as 2.4% in Korea, 4.9% and 5.1% in Japan and the U.S., respectively. The statistics show that the smallest percentage of 8th graders agree that they feel safe a lot at school in Korea than their counterparts in Japan and the U.S.

Approximately, 20% of students in three countries disagree with feeling safe at school, a number significant enough to be noted. Considering the fact that students' self-report is more accurate and reliable than school administrators (Coggeshall & Kingery, 2001; Linares, Díaz, Fuentes, & Acién, 2009), education policymakers and school administrators should take students' reports seriously and utilize the data in developing school violence prevention programs.

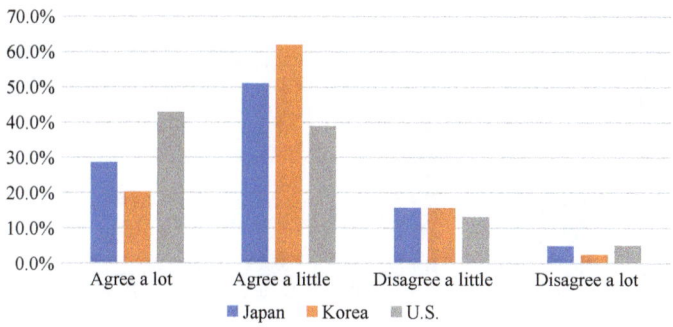

Fig. 3.1 Students' perception on school safety

Teachers' role is critical in preventing and intervening violent incidents. In addition, teachers' stress caused by safety issues negatively influences school outcomes and increases teacher turnover (Smith & Smith, 2006). TIMSS measures teachers' perception of school safety from multiple perspectives. Teachers were given the statement "Thinking about your current school, indicate the extent to which you agree or disagree with each of the following statements: (1) This school is located in a safe neighborhood, (2) I feel safe at this school, (3) This school's security policies and practices are sufficient and (4) The students behave in an orderly manner". The results are presented in Figs. 3.2, 3.3, 3.4, and 3.5 comparing three countries.

Teachers responded to the statement of neighborhood safety around school, and majority of teachers in three countries perceived that their school surroundings are safe: About 95% of Korean teachers, 88% of U.S. teachers, and 87% of Japanese teachers agree a lot or agree a little with the statement. Approximately, 42% of Korean teachers agree a lot that neighborhood of school is safe, whereas 67% of

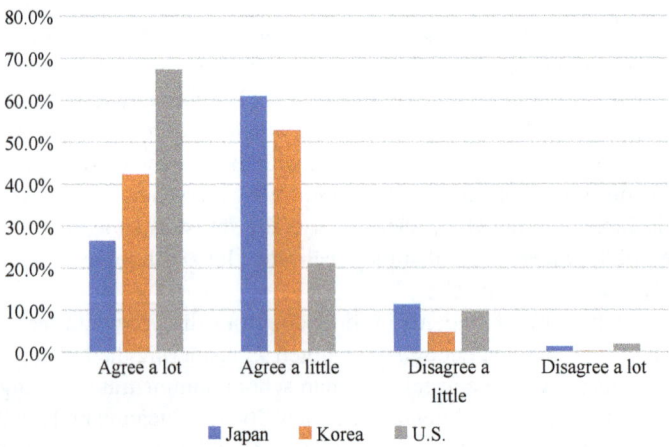

Fig. 3.2 Teachers' perception on school neighborhood safety

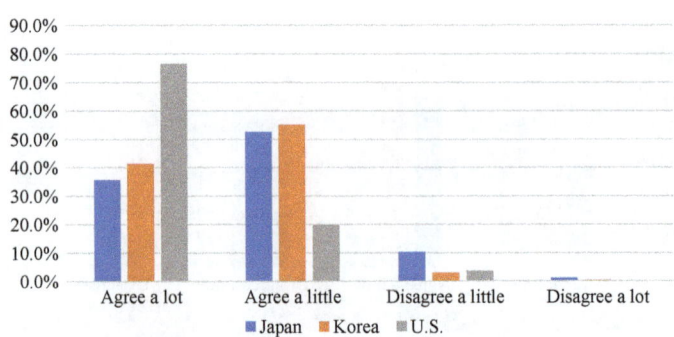

Fig. 3.3 Teachers' perception on school safety

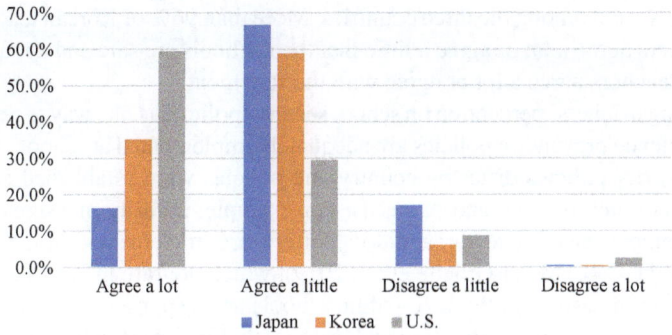

Fig. 3.4 Teachers' perception on school security policies and practices

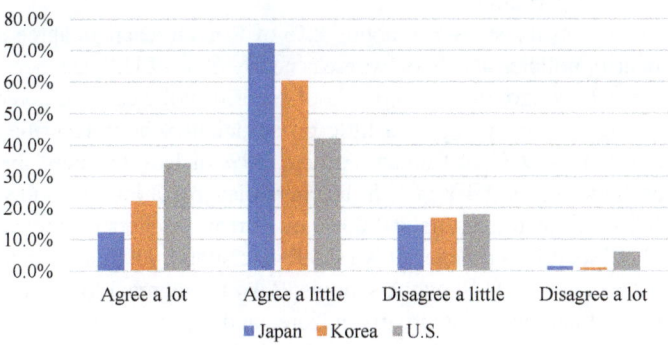

Fig. 3.5 Teachers' perception on students' behavior

U.S. teachers and 26% of Japanese teachers agree a lot with the statement. It is interesting to observe that about 0.3% of teachers at secondary schools disagree a lot about neighborhood safety in Korea, while their counterparts are at 1.3% in Japan and 1.9% in the U.S. In addition, the largest percentage of teachers at secondary schools agree a lot with the statement about neighborhood safety near schools in the U.S.

As mentioned earlier, feeling safe at school is an important indicator in measuring level of school safety. Not only students, but also teachers can also be a target of crime at schools, and such incidents tend to increase. In Korea, despite how teachers are highly respected, there has been an increase in teacher victimization. In the U.S., about 10% of teachers in public school experience threats by a student (Moon & McCluskey, 2016; Musu-Gillette et al., 2019). Therefore, it is worthy to examine teachers' perception on school violence.

TIMSS survey assesses teacher's feeling safe at school, and the results show that about 41% of Korean teachers agree a lot with feeling safe at school, whereas about 36% of Japanese teachers and 76% of U.S. teachers agree a lot with the statement. It is noticeable that the largest percentage of secondary school teachers in the U.S.

feel safe at school among the three countries. More than 96% of Korean teachers and U.S. teachers agree a lot or agree a little that their schools are safe and about 88% of Japanese teachers agree a lot or agree with the statement.

Knowing teachers' perception on school security policies is one way to reveal how school violence prevention policies are adequately implemented at school. Although school security policies differ by country, the policies were established according to the school environment and its needs. For example, security measures, such as security camera, metal detector, and dog sniffers, are implemented in many public schools in the U.S. (Musu-Gillette et al., 2019), which are rare in Korea and Japan. Such security measures in the U.S. public schools are responses to certain types of violent incidents including shooting and drug-related incidents, which are also rare circumstances in Korea and Japan. Despite different security measures and policies in three countries, it is worthy to examine how teachers think about their school's security policies in particular.

TIMSS survey results show that about 35% of Korean teachers agree a lot with sufficient security policies at school, whereas nearly 60% of U.S. teachers and 16% of Japanese teachers agree a lot with school security policies. The percentage of teachers who agree a lot or agree a little on sufficient school securities policies are observed as about 94% of Korean teachers, 89% of U.S. teachers, and 83% of Japanese teachers. About 2.4% of U.S. teachers disagree a lot with the statement, whereas 0.3% of Korean teachers and 0.4% of Korean teachers disagree a lot with sufficient school securities policies. It is a small percentage, yet more than 6 times the percentage of teachers in U.S. public schools (2.4%) disagree a lot about sufficient security policies than their counterparts in Korea and Japan.

Teachers' perception on students' acts of orderly manner was assessed. Classroom disorder caused by students' behaviors might not always be directly linked to violence, yet it promotes a fear of violence among students at secondary schools (Akiba, 2008). TIMSS survey results show that more than 82% of Korean teachers agree a lot or agree a little on students' orderly behavior, whereas 84% of Japanese teachers and 76% of U.S. teachers responded to this question. Percentage of teachers who disagree a lot with students' orderly behaviors is the smallest in Korea (0.9%) as those appear to be 1.3% in Japan and 6% in the U.S. About a quarter of U.S. teachers who participated in the TIMSS survey disagree that students behave in an orderly manner, which is slightly higher than that of Korea and Japan.

It is worthy to understand the differences on classroom and instruction structures among the three countries. In Korea and Japan, students at secondary schools do not change classrooms unless attending required special classes such as music, lab science, and physical education. They stay with the same classmates in the same classroom every school day and study the same subjects on the same schedule. A homeroom teacher ensures the whole learning process from the beginning to the end of the day. Student behaviors are more likely to be the responsibility of their homeroom teacher, which gives more authority to their homeroom teacher. It is common that any incidents are reported to homeroom teacher first and then it may be sent to the principal if the problem cannot be resolved (Akiba & Shimizu, 2013). In addition, teachers in Korea are more likely to believe in teacher-directed classroom management and to utilize disciplinary actions for student behavior management (Koh & Shin, 2014).

Compared to those features in Korea and Japan, secondary schools in the U.S. have classroom changes, independently chosen schedules, and no homeroom teacher, which leaves a lot to the students' own control.

While school principals' report about school violence has been underestimated in terms of its accuracy (Coggeshall & Kingery, 2001), principal's perception provides an important insight to measure school safety. In the TIMSS survey, principals were asked "To what degree is each of the following a problem among eighth grade students in your school?" and were given items related to student problem behaviors. Principals responded to each item based on four scales: not a problem, minor problem, moderate problem, or serious problem. In the analysis, six items about violent student's behaviors (e.g., profanity, vandalism, intimidation, or verbal abuse among students, physical injury to students, intimidation or verbal abuse of teachers or staff, physical injury to teachers or staff) were chosen to compare the degree of school violence in three countries. The percentages were calculated to get the sum of three responses (minor problem, moderate problem, and serious problem).

As shown in Fig. 3.6, intimidations among students and profanity are the most common forms of school violence in Korea. More than 60% of Korean principals perceive intimidation or verbal abuse among students and profanity are problems at school (64% and 63.3%, respectively). A similar pattern of prevalent intimidation among students and profanity is observed in the U.S. (83.6% and 75.8%, respectively), but not in Japan. About 71% of principals in Japan reported intimidations among students, and 39% of principles reported students' physical injury as a problem at school.

The most prevalent type of violence at school in three countries is observed as intimidation and verbal abuse among students. In the TIMSS questionnaire, harmful emailing or texting was considered as intimidation or verbal abuse, which reflects that

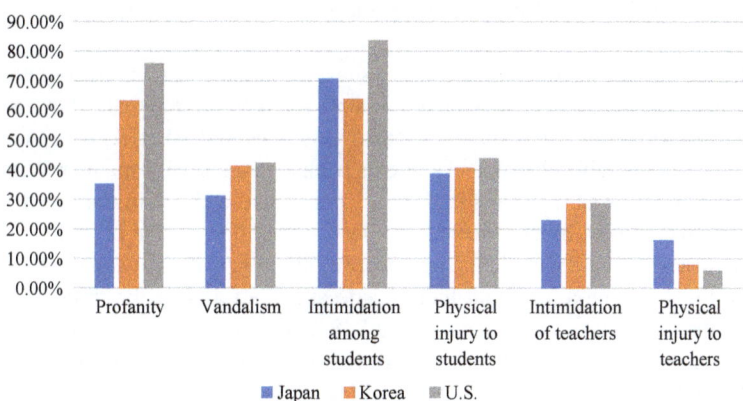

Fig. 3.6 Level of school violence by principals' reports

student's problem behaviors are frequently caused through the Internet and social media.

Bullying incidents occurs in school ground and more easily in virtual environment through the Internet (Reports of school bullying, October 26, 2017). As mentioned, the degree of each form of school violence shows similar patterns in three countries, yet physical injury to teachers and staff was reported by more principals in Japan than their counterparts in Korea and U.S. More than 16% of Japanese principals reported physical injury to teachers and staff, and the percentage is about two times greater than that of Korea and the U.S. (8% and 5.9%).

Overall, principals' perceived school violence shows that Korea has a higher degree of school violence than Japan, but lower than the U.S., except for intimidation among students and physical injury to teachers and staff.

Summary

This chapter has shown a comparison of the perception of students, teachers, and principals regrading school violence in Korea, Japan, and the U.S. Based on the TIMSS survey data, three countries were compared focused on students' perceived safety at school; teachers' perception on safety at school and neighborhood, security policies, and student's behaviors; principals' perception on students' violent behaviors toward students as well as teachers.

In Korea, only one-fifth of the students agree about a lot about feeling safe at school, which is the smallest percentage out of the three countries. Except for one measure (e.g., student's behavior), Korean teachers tend to agree on school safety than their counterparts in Japan, and the U.S. Principals in Korea responded to six types of school violence, and it reveals that intimidation and profanity are the most common at school. It also shows that Korea has school violence incidents fewer than the U.S. but more than Japan, except for intimidation among students and injury to teachers.

Although school violence is a critical issue around the world, an overall majority of students, teachers, and principals in the three countries agree that: They feel safe at school, schools operate adequate security practices and policies, their school is located in a safe neighborhood, and students behave in an orderly manner. With such major agreement on safe schools in Korea, Japan, and the U.S., similar and different tendencies were also observed in stakeholders' perception of school violence in the three countries. From the students' perspective, the largest percentage of students in the U.S. (43%) agree a lot about feeling safe at school among the three countries, whereas the percentage of students in the U.S. and Japan who disagree a lot about feeling safe at school is twice than that of Korea. From the teachers' perspective, more than 96% of Korean and U.S. teachers report feeling safe at school, yet fewer Japanese teachers agreed with the statement (88%). It is noticeable that the largest percentage of U.S. teachers agree a lot in all measures of school safety, school neighborhood safety, security practices, and students' behaviors in an orderly manner than their counterparts in Korea and Japan. Finally, from school principals' perspective, the largest percentage of principals that ranged from 64 to 84% in three countries reported intimidation and verbal abuse among students as a problem out of the six forms of school violence. More than 60 percentage of principals in Korea and the U.S. reported profanity as a problem, whereas only 35% of principals in Japan reported it as a problem.

In summary, perceived school violence in three countries was observed with a similar tendency and small differences. For instance, Korean teachers are more likely to agree about school safety than their counterparts in Japan and the U.S. More students and teachers in the U.S. seem to agree a lot on various measures of school safety compared to their counterparts in Korea and Japan, yet the largest percentage of principals in U.S. reported school violence among students than their counterparts in Korea and Japan. Overall, perceived level of school safety in Japan appears higher than those of Korea and the U.S., yet violent incident to teachers is perceived more problematic. Approximately, 35% of principals in three countries reported intimidation and/or injury toward teachers as a problem at school, yet twice the number of Japanese principals reported teachers' injury as a problem than principals in Korea and the U.S.

References

Agnew, R. (2003). An integrated theory of the adolescent peak in offending. *Youth & Society, 34*(3), 263–299.

Akiba, M. (2008). Predictors of student fear of school violence: a comparative study of eight graders in 33 countries. *School Effectiveness and School Improvement, 19*(1), 51–72.

Akiba, M. (2010). What predicts fear of school violence among U.S. adolescents? *Teachers College Record, 112*(1), 68–102

Akiba, M., & Han, S. (2007). Academic differentiation, school achievement, and school violence in the U.S. and South Korea. *Compare, 37*(2), 201–219.

Akiba, M., & Shimizu, K. (2013). Student-teacher relationship and Ijime in Japanese middle schools. In G. DeCoker & C. Bjork (Eds.), *Japanese education in an era of globalization: Culture, politics, and equity* (pp. 67–81). Teachers College Press

Bear, G., Manning, M. A., & Shiomi, K. (2006). Children's reasoning about aggression: Differences between Japan and the United States and implications for school discipline. *School Psychology Review, 35*(1), 62–77.

Benbenishty, R., & Astor, R. A. (2005). *School violence in context: Culture, neighborhood, family, school, and gender*. Oxford.

Bergmüller, S. (2013). The relationship between cultural individualism–collectivism and student aggression across 62 countries. *Aggressive Behavior, 39*, 182–200.

Chen, Y., Cheng, J., Liang, C., & Sato, M. (2012). Some factors in deviant behaviors of elementary school students in Taiwan and Japan. *Social Behavior and Personality, 40*(4), 623–638.

Coggeshall, M. B., & Kingery, P. M. (2001). Cross-survey analysis of school violence and disorder. *Psychology in the School, 38*(2), 107–116.

Crothers, L. M., Kolbert, J. B., & Barker, W. F. (2006). Middle school students' preferences for anti-bullying interventions. *School Psychology International, 27*(4), 475–487.

Dake, J. A., Price, J. H., Telljohann, S. K., & Funk, J. B. (2003). Teacher perceptions and practices regarding school bullying prevention. *Journal of School Health, 73*(9), 347–355.

Demaray, M. K., Malecki, C. K., Secord, S. M., & Lyell, K. M. (2013). Agreement among students', teachers', and parents' perceptions of victimization by bullying. *Children and Youth Services Review, 35,* 2091–2100.

Hara, H. (2002). Justifications for bullying among Japanese school children. *Asian Journal of Social Psychology, 5,* 197–204.

Harris, S., & Hathorn, C. (2006). Texas middle school principals' perceptions of bullying on campus. *The National Association of Secondary School Principals Bulletin, 90*(1), 49–69.

Johnson, S. L., Waasdorp, T. E., Gaias, L. M., & Bradshaw, C. P. (2019). Parental responses to bullying: Understanding the role of school policies and practices. *Journal of Educational Psychology, 111*(3), 475–487.

Kanetsuna, T., & Smith, P. K. (2002). Pupil insights into bullying and coping with bullying: A bi-national study in Japan and England. *Journal of School Violence, 1*(3), 5–29.

Kearney, W. S., & Smith, P. (2018). Student bullying, teacher protection, and administrator role ambiguity: A multi-level analysis of elementary schools. *Journal of School Leadership, 28*(3), 374–400.

Klein, J. (2012). *The bully society: School shootings and the crisis of bullying in America's schools.* New York University.

Kobayashi, E., & Farrington, D. (2020). Why do Japanese bully more than Americans? Influence of external locus of control and student attitudes toward bullying. *Educational Science: Theory and Practice., 20*(1), 5–19.

Koh, M., & Shin, S. (2014). A comparative study of elementary teachers' beliefs and strategies on classroom and behavior management in the USA and Korean school systems. *International Journal of Progressive Education, 10*(3), 18–33.

Korean Educational Development Institute. (2005). *Educational issues monitoring survey results.* Retrieved August 30, 2020, from https://www.kedi.re.kr/khome/main/webhome/Home.do

Kwon, S., & Kim, T. (2015). On school violence in Korean middle school, prevention, and reaction measures. *Journal of Exercise Rehabilitation, 11*(1), 41–47. https://doi.org/10.12965/jer.150184.

Lee, S., Smith, P. K., & Monks, C. P. (2011). Perceptions of bullying-like phenomena in South Korea: a qualitative approach from a life span perspective. *Journal of Aggression, Conflict and Peach Research, 3*(4), 210–221.

Lerner, D. (2011). *Cyberbullying among children in Japanese and American middle schools: An exploration of prevalence and predictors* (Unpublished master's thesis). Arizona State University.

Linares, J. J. G., Díaz, A. J. C., Fuentes, M. D. C. P., & Acién, F. L. (2009). Teachers' perception of school violence in a sample from three European countries. *European Journal of Psychology of Education, 24*(1), 49–59.

Longobardi, C., Lotti, N. O., Jungert, T., & Settanni, M. (2018). Student-teacher relationships and bullying: The role of student social status. *Journal of Adolescence, 63,* 1–10.

Moon, B., & McCkuskey, J. (2016). School-based victimization of teachers in Korea: Focusing on individual and school characteristics. *Journal of Interpersonal Violence, 31*(7), 1340–1361.

Mucherah, W., Finch, H., White, T., & Thomas, K. (2018). The relationship of school climate, teacher defending and friends on students' perceptions of bullying in high school. *Journal of Adolescence, 62,* 128–139.

Musu-Gillette, L., Zhang, A., Wang, K., Zhang, J., & Oudekerk, B. A. (2017). *Indicators of school crime and safety: 2016* (NCES 2017-064/NCJ 250650). National Center for Education Statistics, U.S. Department of Education, and Bureau of Justice Statistics, Office of Justice Programs, U.S. Department of Justice. Retrieved August 30, 2020, from https://nces.ed.gov/pubs2017/2017064.pdf

Musu-Gillette, L., Zhang, A., Wang, K., Zhang, J., & Oudekerk, B. A. (2019). *Indicators of school crime and safety: 2018.* National Center for Education Statistics, U.S. Department of Education, and Bureau of Justice Statistics, Office of Justice Programs, U.S. Department of Justice. Retrieved August 30, 2020, from https://www.bjs.gov/content/pub/pdf/iscs18.pdf

National Center for Injury Prevention and Control. (2016). *Understating school violence.* Retrieved August 30, 2020, from https://www.cdc.gov/violenceprevention/pdf/School_Violence_Fact_S heet-a.pdf

Norwalk, K. E., Hamm, J. V., Farmer, T. W., & Barnes, K. L. (2015). Improving the school context of early adolescence through teacher attunement to victimization: Effects on school belonging. *Journal of Early Adolescence, 1*(21), 989–1009.

Organisation for Economic Co-operation and Development (OECD). (2017). *Programme for International Students Assessment (PISA) results from PISA 2015 Students' Well-Being.* Retrieved August 30, 2020, from OECD.org

Ohbuchi, K., & Kondo, H. (2015). Psychological analysis of serious juvenile violence in Japan. *Asian Criminology, 10,* 149–162.

Park, H., Lee, H., Choi, B., Yu, H., Choi, J., Yoon, A., & Yang, K. (2014). *Hakgyopokruk yebang-moonhwa jungchack bangahn yonku (1)* [A study on school violence prevention culture (1)]. Korean Educational Development Institute. RR2014-33

Park, S., Lee, Y., Jang, H., & Jo, M. (2017). Violence victimization in Korean adolescents: Risk factors and psychological problems. *International Journal of Environmental Research and Public Health, 14*(541), 1–11. https://doi.org/10.3390/ijerph14050541.

Reports of school bullying in Japan rise to record high, education ministry survey shows. (2017, October 26). Retrieved August 30, 2020, from https://www.japantimes.co.jp/news/2017/10/26/national/social-issues/reports-school-bullying-japan-rise-record-high-education-ministry-sur vey-shows/#.WlkKVainGUk

Report of school bullying in Japan up 180%. (2013, December 10). Retrieved August 30, 2020, from https://www.japantimes.co.jp/news/2013/12/10/national/reports-of-school-bullying-in-japan-up-180/#.Wlkoo6inGUk

Sawyer, J., Mishna, F., Pepler, D., & Wiener, J. (2011). The missing voice: Parents' perspectives of bullying. *Children and Youth Services Review, 33,* 1795–1803.

Sims, C. (2001). *Japanese children get scary lessons in fighting violence.* Retrieved August 30, 2020, from https://www.nytimes.com/2001/07/01/world/japanese-children-get-scary-lessons-in-fighting-violence.html

Smith, D. L., & Smith, B. J. (2006). Perceptions of violence: The views of teachers who left urban schools. *High School Journal, 89*(3), 34–42.

Statistics Korea. (2014). *Youth statistics 2014.* Retrieved August 30, 2020, from http://kostat.go.kr

Srabstein, J. C., & Merrick, J. (Eds.). (2013). *Bullying: A public health concern.* Nova Science Pub Inc.

Why bullying in Japanese schools is especially traumatic. (April 12, 2017). *The Economist.* Retrieved August 30, 2020, from https://www.economist.com/news/asia/21720643-evacuees-fuk ushima-are-latest-suffer-torment-class-why-bullying-japanese-schools

Yoon, J., Bauman, S., Choi, T., & Hutchinson, A. S. (2011). How South Korean teachers handle an incident of school bullying. *School Psychology International., 32*(3), 312–329.

Chapter 4
National Characteristics and School Violence

School violence is a critical problem around the world, and this global issue has called for investigation from various perspectives (Benbenishty & Astor, 2008). While many researchers have examined school violence at the individual or school levels, there are small number of studies about school violence from an international perceptive (Akiba, LeTendre, Baker, & Goesling, 2002). While school violence is a common issue in many countries, its frequency and patterns differ across countries. Having knowledge of national characteristics, such as demographics, economic status, and the education system, is beneficial to gain a better understanding the school violence phenomenon.

In this chapter, demographic background, economic status, and education system in Korea, Japan, and the U.S. are presented with school violence by conducting literature reviews and analyzing multiple international datasets. Secondly, the most common types of crime were selected, and each country's rates are compared. Finally, national spending on education, selected national economic indicators, school violence, and delinquency in the three countries are presented. Those indicators are often mentioned as major causes of crime in general strain theory. According to general strain theory (Agnew & White, 1992), criminal acts are caused by three situations: as a threat (1) to prevent you from reaching valued goals, (2) to remove positively valued stimuli, and (3) to present you negatively valued stimuli such as physical assault or verbal abuse. These circumstances can occur in many different contexts, yet this chapter focuses on the impact of the demographic background, economic status, and education system.

Demographic Characteristics and School Violence

Some researchers seek associated factors of school violence from demographic characteristics at the national level. Those factors include, but are not limited to, gender, percentage of the younger population, pattern of population distribution,

© Springer Nature Singapore Pte Ltd. 2021
S. Han, *School Violence in South Korea*,
https://doi.org/10.1007/978-981-16-2730-9_4

ethnic minority group, socioeconomic status, and marital status. In this section, those factors in Korea, Japan, and the U.S. are addressed. While the economic status is often examined as a significant linkage to crime, there is little agreement on the relationship between economic factors and crime. Economic status will be addressed more in detail in the next section.

Before comparing the demographic statistics in Korea, Japan, and the U.S., it is worthy to understand the similarities and differences of tradition, culture, and society among the three countries. To state briefly, Korea and Japan are collectivist, whereas the U.S. is an individualist nation. Under this main difference, both Korea and Japan have been considered as having centralized education system, being ethnically homogeneous societies, and respecting family hierarchy under Confucianism. On the contrary, the U.S. has been considered as having a decentralized education system, being ethnically diverse society, and having nuclear family structure/family instability (Akiba et al., 2002; Bax, 2016; Benbenishty & Astor, 2008; Kang, 2010; Lee, 2001; OECD, 2019a, 2019b; Shin & Koh, 2005). Some of those factors have been rapidly changed in Korea and Japan, yet those factors are fundamental differences from the U.S.

Research has shown that a larger proportion of young people in the population might be linked to the increase of crime. International data showed that the U.S. has about five percent more young population than Korea and Japan. As of 2018, 12.9% of the Korean population is young (less than 15 years old), whereas Japan has 12.2%, and the U.S. has 18.6% of this young population (OECD, 2020b). In addition, crime studies have shown more prevalent crime rates in urban areas than rural or non-urban areas. Population distribution in urban regions differs among Korea, Japan, and the U.S. Korea has more population in urban regions than Japan and the U.S.; Korea has the largest population in urban areas among the three countries. As of 2014, in Korea, 69.6% of the population resides in the urban region, whereas 56.5% in Japan and 42.1% in the U.S. do so. For reference, the average population in urban areas among the OECD countries is 48.2% (OECD, 2020a).

While there is no firm agreement on whether ethnic diversity is related to crime rate, having ethnic diversity changes society in many ways. There has been a considerably large increase of immigrant population in Korea in the past several years. According to the OECD data, as of 2017, Korea has 1.2 million people who were born in another country, such as China, Vietnam, and Uzbekistan. This number is composed of two percent of the population, and it increased 46% since 2007. As the statistics show, Korea has a significant increase in the foreign-born population, and such an increase is the largest among the three countries. Japan had a foreign-born population of 2.6 million in 2018, and main countries are China, Korea, and Vietnam. The number is composed of two percent of the population, and it increased 19% since 2007. As known, the U.S. is the one of the most ethnically diverse countries, and the percentage of foreign-born population is more than six times larger than those of Korea and Japan. The U.S. has 44.5 million people who are foreign-born as of 2018, main countries being Mexico, India, and China. The number is composed of 13% of the population, and it increased 17% since 2007 (OECD, 2019a). The three countries all share ethnic diversity in the society, yet different views were observed across countries. Citizens in Korea and the U.S. tend to be more supportive of ethnic diversity than citizens in Japan. Survey data from 30,133 people in 27 countries showed that more than half of participating Korean and U.S. citizens consider increasing diversity as a positive change (Korea 68% and U.S. 61%), whereas less than half (about 43%) of participating Japanese citizens thought so (Poushter & Fetterolf, 2019). Ethnic diversity is a common experience in many countries, and researchers have examined whether it has impact on violence (Avison & Loring, 1986; Churchill & Laryea, 2019; Lane & Meeker, 2000; Soysa & Noel, 2020; Wadsworth, 2010). Some criminological theorists and social disorganization theorists argue that ethnic and cultural diversity increase violent crime. That is, conflict between subcultural and main cultural group causes violence, and subcultural diversity promotes fear of crime and gang violence (Lane & Meeker, 2000). In addition, a higher level of ethnic diversity is more likely to promote the impact of inequal income on homicide rates (Avison & Loring, 1986). In contrast, others, based on data of more than 140 countries, found little convincing evidence in ethnic diversity as a contributor of social dislocation and homicide (Soysa & Noel, 2020), and data from 78 countries shows that ethnic and linguistic diversity even reduce crime rates (Churchill & Laryea, 2019).

Gender is another leading factor in crime studies. Gender differences in educational outcomes are observed in behavioral and academic outcomes. Previous researchers have demonstrated a significant relationship between academic achievement and problem behaviors, and it is worth acknowledging difference in the patterns among gender, academic achievement, and behavioral outcomes. Academic achievement is observed differently between male and female students in the different subjects in the international tests. The Programme for International Student Assessment (PISA) found male students outperformed in math while female students outperformed in reading, and these patterns are consistently observed in Korea, Japan, and the U.S. Regarding math scores, the average scores are as follows: 528 for male students and 524 for female students in Korea, 532 for male students and 522 for female students in Japan, and 482 for male students and 474 for female students in the U.S. Regarding reading scores, average scores are as follows: 503 for male students and 526 for female students in Korea, 493 for male students and 514 for female students in Japan, and 494 for male students and 517 for female students in the U.S. (OECD, 2018a). In all three countries, male students outperformed female students in mathematics, and female students outperformed male students in reading subjects. In addition, researchers have observed more violent behaviors among male students than female students in Korea, Japan, and the U.S., in the international context (Akiba, Shimizu, & Zhuang, 2010; Fleming & Jacobsen, 2009; Kim, Boyce, Koh, & Leventhal, 2009; Lai, Ye, & Chang, 2008; Long & Dowdell, 2018). Not only gender differences, but gender equality is another issue, and its support differs by country. Data of 27 countries showed that Korea has a larger support for promoting gender equality than Japan and the U.S.; about 75% of participants in Korean strongly supported gender equality, the U.S. had 71% of participants showing such support, whereas only 55% of participating Japanese showed such support (Poushter & Fetterolf, 2019).

Family structure and marital status are important indicators in explaining school violence. A lack of parental support and supervision has been demonstrated as critical factors that contribute to youth crime (Flanagan, Auty, & Farrington, 2019; Mednick, Reznick, Hocevar, & Baker, 1987). In Korea, the relationship between parents and their child is highly valued within collectivism. Strong parent–child bonds are considered an important factor for a household. Korean parents are actively involved in their child's education; as international data shows, 97% of Korean students reported having parents who are interested in their school activities (OECD, 2017). Research shows that children with divorced parents are more likely to have stress and less likely to receive adequate supervision and attention. Such a situation might make a child vulnerable to involvement in violent behaviors. Empirical studies found a positive relationship between parental divorce and youth crime (Mednick et al., 1987; Sirvanli-Ozen, 2008; Weaver, & Schofield, 2015), and conflicts among family members might be linked to physical assault (Felson, Osgood, Horney, & Wiernik, 2012). Family data in OECD countries shows the distinct patterns in divorce rates across countries. As of 2017, the divorce rate per 1,000 people is 2.1% in Korea. Among the three countries, Japan has the lowest divorce rate, and the U.S. has the highest divorce rate (1.7% and 2.9%, respectively). Another indicator of family structure is the percentage of sharing births with those born outside of marriage out of all births. As of 2014, Korea has 1.9% of children born outside the marriage are shared in a family, and 2.3% in Japan and 40.2% in the U.S., respectively (OECD, 2020b). Such situations result from changes in living patterns among the young generation. Young people are less likely to marry and more likely to cohabit. In addition, even some married couples tend to get divorced. Such non-traditional partnership and divorce tend to be more common among young people, and these factors increase the number of children who are born outside marriage (OECD, 2011). Children in single-parent or altered family structures are more at risk in terms of receiving less than adequate degree of care and supervision and less likely to have sound bonding with family members.

Comparison of demographic characteristics in the three countries showed that Korea and Japan have similar proportions of young people out of the entire population, family divorce rates, and the rate of having children outside of marriages than the U.S. It is noticeable that Korea has a larger urban population and a rapid increase of ethnic diversity than Japan and the U.S. In addition, the U.S. has about five times larger of a proportion of young people in the population than Korea and Japan, and the U.S. also has about six times more ethnically diverse population than Korea and Japan. Divorce rate in the U.S. is higher than that of Korea and Japan, yet a more distinguished feature is that about 20 times larger percentage of sharing children outside of marriage in the U.S. than Japan and Korea. These demographic differences in Korea, Japan, and the U.S. provide a good background information that sets a solid foundation to understand school violence phenomenon at the international level, particularly when the distinguished national features are known as significant linkages to school violence.

Economic Circumstances and School Violence

Many researchers seek predictors of school violence from economic status. Major crime theories and a number of studies attempted to investigate a relationship between crime and poverty (Baron, 2007; Felson et al., 2012; Pratt, & Lowenkamp, 2002; Rosenfeld, 2009).

Prior to addressing the relationship between crime and economic status, it is important to understand how economic status is measured in the empirical studies. Economic status in research is measured by various methods. School lunch status (percent of students who are eligible for free and/or reduced-price lunch) is one of the most frequently used indicators of economic status of a household in education research. Parent's income level, parents' professions, and social status are also used as student's economic indicators in education studies. At the national level, there are economic indicators that were often used in crime studies: national gross domestic product per capita to assess national wealth and Gini coefficient to assess income inequality (Akiba et al., 2002; Corcoran, Pettinicchio, & Robbins, 2018; Elgar, Craig, Boyce, Morgan, & Vella-Zarb, 2009). Many researchers have demonstrated a link between economic status and crime, yet there is little consensus on the relationship. Extensive literature review revealed that income inequality and poverty are respectively associated with crime, yet the estimated size of relationships vary. In addition, types of crime have different linkages with economic status. Assault and homicide, rather than robbery and rape, are more likely to associated with income equality or poverty (Hsieh & Pugh, 1993). Another literature review on 273 studies showed that violent crime and delinquency are more likely to correlate with individual social status, rather than parent's social status, and drug-related offenses significantly, positively correlate with parent's social status (Lee & McDonald, 2001). Some researchers argue that distribution of wealth is an important predictor of violence, yet the findings are inconsistent across studies. Elgar et al. (2009) found a significant association between income inequality and bullying rates based on the data of 66,910 students in 37 countries. They concluded that adolescents might have more bullying problems in countries with higher income inequality than countries with lower income inequality. Akiba et al. (2002) analyzed the data of students in 37 countries and found that school violence (e.g., student victimization and peer victimization) is more connected to poverty levels, rather than income disparity within a nation. Corcoran et al. (2018) analyzed data of 100 countries including a nationally representative survey data of residents who are 15 years old or older. They found that income inequality was more likely to increase intentional homicides, but no statistically significant link between income inequality and assault was observed. Another study, analyzing data of 37 countries, reveals predictors of different types of crime including violent crime, property crime, alcohol abuse, and drug use. Social inequality, lack of social control, and prevalent material poverty are significant predictors of violent crime, whereas urbanization and wealthy context with leisure-oriented lifestyle are significantly related to alcohol and drug use (Eisner, 2002).

Although previous studies give us mixed findings on the relationship among income inequality, poverty level, and crime, the data of perception of economic status give us an interesting assumption. OECD provides data about proportion of economically vulnerable people in countries. An indicator of individuals who are economically vulnerable was measured as the percentage of people who cannot live above the poverty line for three consecutive months if their income suddenly stops. According to the OECD Wealth Distribution database, Korea has 4.3%, Japan has 13.6%, and the U.S. has 36.5% of such economically vulnerable individuals, while the average percentage of such people among OECD countries is 35.7% as of 2015 (OECD, 2019b). As we review crime and school violence in the literature, Korea and Japan have much lower rates of school violence than that of the U.S. This indicator, percent of economically vulnerable people, showed that the U.S. has more than eight times larger percent of economically vulnerable people than Korea. There should be more discussion on economic impact on crime, yet this gives us another way to measure economic status in examining the relationship with crime.

While many studies seek predictors of crime from economic factors, there are mixed findings and very few studies focusing on school violence and economic status at the national-level studies. As mentioned earlier, there are various measures on economic status, and it would be beneficial to utilize multiple measures for a student and their family's economic status. In addition, previous studies showed that different types of crime have different correlations with economic status. Some studies showed that serious crime, such as homicide, is positively related to poverty, yet drug problems are indirectly related to poverty and is even negatively related to poverty in some context. Furthermore, school violence itself is also measured in different ways. While some studies measure school violence as serious crime, such as homicide and rape, other studies assess school violence in a broader sense, ranging from physical fight to classroom disruption. To explore the relationship between school violence and economic status, utilizing various measures on economic status and differentiating type of violence should be prerequisites.

School System and School Violence

School system has been examined to see whether a certain aspect of education system is associated with school violence or how certain education systems promote safer learning environments. Many researchers have examined how school factors including, but are not limited to, centralized vs. decentralized education system, class size, school size, teacher–student ratio, differentiated tracking system, discipline policies, and quality of teachers are linked to school violence. In this section, national indicators on education system and school violence are presented by utilizing previous empirical studies and international data sources.

The Korean education system has been developed as a modern education system during the Japanese colonial period from 1910 to 1945. In 1948, the Republic of Korea, new government, established the current Korean education system based on the U.S. education system (Shin, & Koh, 2005). Historically, Korean modern education system has been influenced both by Japan and the U.S. and maintains the 6 (elementary)-3, (middle)-3, and (high)-4 (post-secondary) system.

Regarding school systems, one of the most challenging issues is probably to achieve both excellence and equity. Students should receive quality education with equal learning opportunities regardless of their individual characteristics, such as gender, socioeconomic status, or ethnicity. Although an education system is built to achieve such goals, there are many barriers.

According to the general strain theory, being in a low socioeconomic status prevents one from desired goals (higher achievement or not being punished) (Agnew & White, 1992). It is commonly known that students from more wealthier homes or wealthy school areas are more likely to perform better than their counterparts from poor homes or poor school areas. Academic achievement is also measured as one of the indicators of an effective school system (Akiba et al., 2002), and it is interesting to see how economic factors are related to a school system. International data shows that the impact of socioeconomic status on academic achievement differs among countries at the national level. Among OECD countries, socioeconomic status predicts more than 15% in reading performance in 20 countries and less than 10% in 31 countries. On average, the socioeconomic status predicts less than 15% of mathematics and science performance in OECD countries (13.8% in mathematics performance and 12.8% in science performance). Some countries have a stronger impact of socioeconomic status on academic performance than other countries and more than 20% of mathematics performance were predicted by socioeconomic status in seven countries. In terms of this measure, socioeconomic has a smaller impact on academic achievement in Korea and Japan compared to the U.S. (OECD, 2019c).

Researchers have demonstrated that socioeconomic status has impact on student's behavioral outcomes and/or discipline practices. National samples of the U.S. revealed that socioeconomic status influences discipline practices. Research showed that schools that serve more disadvantaged students (e.g., students from poor family, ethnic minority, and underachievers) are more likely to take serious disciplinary actions than their counterparts (Han & Akiba, 2011; Skiba, Michael, Nardo, & Peterson, 2002). It is naturally assumed that disciplinary actions result from students' behavior, yet many research studies show that frequent disciplinary practices and harsh security policies might be related to the school's poverty level and a student's disadvantaged status. Schools that serve more disadvantaged students tend to take more disciplinary actions than schools serving fewer disadvantaged students, even when the schools have the same level of problem behaviors (Han & Akiba, 2011; Welsh & Little, 2018), and schools that serve more non-White students and poor students are more likely to implement harsher security policies (Aaron & Ward, Aaron and Ward 2014). Every nation attempts to establish a better school system that offers students quality education, equal opportunity, and a safer learning environment. It is critical for school administrators and policymakers to improve education system in a fair and effective manner and minimize negative impact from outside factors including economic factors.

Probably, one of the most well-known features in the Korean education system is its extremely competitive education (Dawson, 2010; Kwon, Lee, & Shin, 2017). Such competitive education, called "education fever," is not a unique phenomenon in Korea, but it has been a common issue in many developed countries including Japan (Nakamura, 2005). Since 1948, the Korean government vigorously initiated educational development, which promoted rapid economic development toward becoming industrialized country. Such expansion of educational opportunity to the public stimulated parents' enthusiasm in the involvement of their child's education to pursue upward social status and economic mobility. This situation is often expressed as "education fever" or "education zeal" (Lee, Lee, & Jang, 2010; Seth, 2012).

Although the Korean education system has been reformed for a well-rounded education, preparation for college entrance exams remains a crucial issue. "Examination hell," referring to a student's life extensively studying, especially during the high school years, with very limited family, social, and leisure time, is observed in Korea, Japan, and many other East Asian countries (Nakamura, 2003; OECD, 2018b). About 75% of Korean students pursue a college degree (OECD, 2017), and the college entrance exam is offered once a year with limited number of college applications. Many students pursue prestigious colleges, and if they fail to receive admission, students need to re-take the college exam the next school year. It is strongly believed that a degree from a prestigious college guarantees a better future, thus getting into those colleges has a significant influence on the entire education process in Korea. Such circumstances have resulted from many factors including the government's strong regulation on education under a centralized education system, equalized secondary school system, and hierarchical higher education system based on prestigious colleges (Kim & Lee, 2010).

Being raised in the competitive learning environment in Korea has its positive effects. Korean students study hard, build confidence through schooling, and are highly motivated academically. As shown in the international data, about 82% of Korean students want to be the best in the class (OECD, 2017). Despite the positive aspects, this exam preparation-oriented education results in many serious problems not limited to rote learning, considerable expenses for cram school and private tutors, stress, anxiety, and pressure from extreme competition. Although Korean students outperformed in the multiple international tests, they are less satisfied with their life and feel anxious about their schoolwork. International data sources showed that only 18.6% of Korean students reported being very satisfied with life, and 42% of Korean students reported becoming tense when studying. Spending too many hours studying causes lack of physical exercise as well. Less than half of Korean students (46.3%) reported exercising or playing sports before or after school (OECD, 2017). Such competitive learning environment damages students' well-rounded education in this way, and this problem is critical both in Korea and Japan. Lee (2001) asserted that the education system in Korea and Japan have been more likely to focus mainly on academic achievement and national development. Such education system considerably contributes building human capital and economic development. At the same time, school education is degraded only to the means of college entrance preparation, which also damages humane education and students' interest in learning (Lee, 2001).

Students under such an education system perceive and act differently from their counterparts under a contrasting education system in Western countries. A comparative study in Korea and the U.S. revealed that academic tracking system, which offers different curriculum to different group of academic ability, is a significant predictor of school violence in Korea, but not in the U.S. This finding implies that Korean students might perceive themselves as inferior than their counterparts in an outperforming academic group. Students who develop a negative self-image and perceive a lack of learning opportunity might cause conflict with peers, and these individuals are more likely to be involved in violent incidents (Akiba & Han, 2007). In addition, extremely competitive learning environment can be a barrier in developing friendship as students tend to perceive their peers as competitors. Research revealed that having poor-quality friendship is linked to delinquent behavior later in life among Korean adolescents (Cho & Galehan, 2020). Competition in school causes stress among students, and this leads to more serious problems. Data of 569 Korean high school students showed that students' school-related stress is a significant and direct predictor of suicidal ideation (Kim, Moon, Lee, & Kim, 2018).

Different features in instruction structure and discipline practices in secondary schools are observed among Korea, Japan, and the U.S. In Korea and Japan, disciplining students is mostly the classroom teacher's responsibility. Minor problem behavior is addressed within the classroom, and students are sent to the faculty office or have their parents contacted only in cases of more serious problem behaviors, which can result in suspension. In Korea and Japan, teachers are considered to have equal authority as parents, and such respect is applied not only to discipline practice but in teaching the students in the classroom. Both in Korea and Japan, students have a homeroom teacher and the same classmates for one school year. It could be easier to build bonds with homeroom teacher and peers, compared to those in the U.S. education system. On the other hand, students might need to make more effort to get along with classmates as they go through together for the entire school year. Research show that students who have a strong bond with teachers are less likely to become victim to bullying and tend to share the same value regarding school rules. In addition, students are less likely to fear becoming a victim where teachers emphasize their efforts to understand students (Akiba & Han, 2007; Akiba et al., 2010; Shin & Koh, 2005). Thus, it is essential for school administrators and policymakers to develop an education system to improve bonds between teachers and students, which impact students' academic and behavioral outcomes. Although modern Korean society changes rapidly, there are still influences of Confucianism and respect for hierarchy. Educational context is affected such influences, and the hierarchy between teacher and students and between senior and younger students remains today. For example, in Korea, it is common that selected senior students monitor younger students' behaviors in the mornings and in hallways in general (Shin & Koh, 2005).

International survey data shows the differences in satisfaction and confidence of a country on its education system in multiple countries. More than half of the citizens in Korea, Japan, and the U.S. are satisfied with their education systems. Koreans are the least satisfied with their education system, and U.S. citizens are the most satisfied with their education system. In 2018, based on Gallop World Poll data, about 51% of Korean citizens were satisfied and felt confident about the education system, whereas 59% of citizens in Japan and 64% of citizens in the U.S. were satisfied and felt confident (the average is 66% for OECD countries responding with such satisfaction and confidence). (OECD, 2019b).

There is little consensus about the linkage between certain characteristics of education systems and school violence in literature. However, the Korean education system might have potential risk factors that intimidate school safety. As addressed earlier, strong education regulations by the government produce a uniform school system, which leads to more standardized education and assessment. Uniform secondary schools and hierarchical higher education systems lead to extreme competition for admission to prestigious colleges, which cause various problems. Students have stress for preparing for college entrance exams and have challenges developing friendships in such competitive culture. Having academic stress and poor relationships with peers might develop conflicts among peers, result in delinquent behavior or even suicidal ideation and attempt. While these circumstances are rarely observed in the U.S., there are potential risk factors in instruction structure and discipline practices in the U.S. that might contribute to the prevalence of school violence. Compared to secondary schools in Korea and Japan, U.S. secondary schools give more opportunities to students to exercise students' autonomy. Without having homeroom teachers, students choose their own subjects for the school year and change classrooms each period according to their schedule. While this instruction structure develops a student's independence, it could offer fewer opportunities to build bonding with teachers and peers. In addition, classroom changes might cause potential conflicts among students while moving between classrooms. Regarding discipline practices, in the U.S., disciplinary actions are implemented mainly by school principals rather than teachers. In Korea and Japan, the homeroom teacher is essentially responsible for disciplining students with its reasoning being that homeroom teachers knows most about the students and the setting and circumstances where problem behaviors occur. Discipline practices in the U.S. could be reformed in emphasizing bonding between teachers and students as well as in minimizing potential conflicts among students in its instruction structure.

In summary, school systems in Korea, Japan, and the U.S. have been developed in different historical and cultural backgrounds, yet all those education systems attempt to achieve better outcomes in academical and behavioral aspects. While all education systems pursue similar goals in different countries, an education system can cause extreme academic competition among students, promote a stronger bonding between teachers and students, minimize conflicts among students based on instruction structures, and reduce economic impact on students' academic achievement. There are many potential factors that we can consider in reducing school violence in all different education systems in Korea, Japan, and the U.S.

Comparison of National Characteristics and School Violence in Korea, Japan, and the U.S.

There are widespread assumptions that crime in society could be related to youth crime. Many researchers have examined how adult crime is related to delinquency (Akiba et al., 2002; Mason et al., 2010). While there is no firm consensus on the relationship between adult crime and youth crime, it is worthy to examine crime rate along with school violence in Korea, Japan, and the U.S.

Crime rates in Korea, Japan, and the U.S. are presented here based on the data of United Nations Statistics, 2014 or latest data. Six forms of crime were chosen for comparison, which causes serious physical harm as well as were considered as "traditional" crime types (Harrendorf, Heiskanen, & Malby, 2010). Data is based on the United Nations Statistics resources (United Nations Office on Drugs and Crime, 2018), and each type of crime was measured per 100,000 population.

Figure 4.1 shows that theft, burglary, and assault are the most common out of six types of crime in the three countries. In Korea, rate of theft is at 531.65, burglary at 160.4, and assault at 100.41. Rates of more serious crime are relatively low compared to the types mentioned above. Rate of rape is at 13.36, and robbery and homicide are at 3.17 and 0.74, respectively. These patterns of crime are consistently observed in Japan and the U.S., yet the rates of those crimes in Korea are higher than rates of Japan and lower than rates of the U.S. It is noticeable that crime rates are the highest in all six types of crime in the U.S. than those of Korea and those of Japan. For the rate of theft, the U.S. is at 1773.4, which is three times more than Korea and four times more than Japan. For the rate of burglary, the U.S. is at 490.88, which is three times more than Korea and six time more than Japan. For the rate of assault, the U.S. is at 237.57, which is about two times more than Korea and ten times more than Japan.

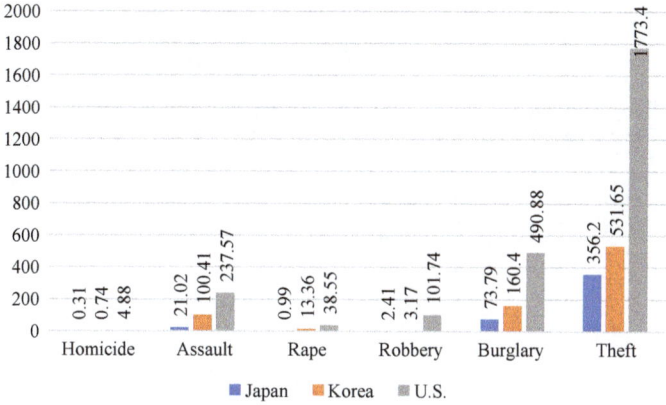

Fig. 4.1 Crime rates in Japan, Korea, and the U.S.

The patterns and prevalence of crime in Korea, Japan, and the U.S. are observed similarly with those of school violence, which is the highest in the U.S. and the lowest in Japan among the three countries (see Chapter 2). On the other hand, it is also interesting to see how each country has satisfaction with and confidence in their police service. The Gallop World Poll database showed that 67% of Korean citizens felt satisfied and confident with the country's police service, whereas 72% of Japanese citizens, 79% of U.S. citizens and 77% of citizens of OECD countries felt satisfied and confident with their respective countries' police service (OECD, 2019b). The data examined here seems to imply that countries with more prevalent crime have a higher level of satisfaction and confidence with police service than countries with fewer incidents of crime. Although the U.S. has the highest crime rate compared to Korea and Japan, the largest percentage of U.S. citizens are satisfied and confident with police service among the three countries.

As mentioned earlier, there are empirical research studies focusing on the relationship between delinquency and adult crime. Some researchers assert that delinquency is closely related to adult crime and others are little convinced with such assertion along with inconclusive empirical findings. Akiba et al. (2002) examined the relationship between school violence and crime rates in 37 countries. In their study, school violence was measured by student victimization, peer victimization, classroom disruption, and classroom threat. Crime rates are measured for homicide, rape, robbery, assault, threat, and sexual offenses. The findings showed that correlational analysis between four types of school violence and crime rates revealed no statistically significant correlations (Akiba et al., 2002).

Figure 4.2 shows the comparison of national characteristics by three categories: education, economic status, and violence/delinquency. The data was collected from international data resources from the Organisation for Economic Co-operation and

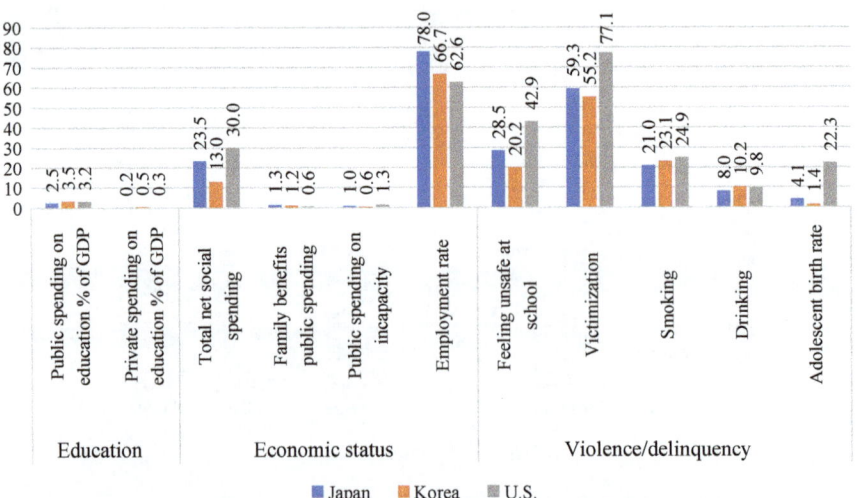

Fig. 4.2 Comparison of national characteristics and student victimization

Development (OECD) and World Health Organization (WHO) in 2015 or latest available.

For the education category, two indicators were included: public spending on education as percent of GDP and private spending on education as percent of GDP. Public spending on education refers to "direct expenditure on educational institutions as well as educational-related public subsidies given to households and administered by educational institutions" and private spending on education refers to "expenditure funded by private sources which are households and other private entities." Both public and private spending on education were measured as percent of GDP and include primary to post-secondary both non-tertiary and tertiary as of 2016. All data and descriptions about education spending are based on OECD data (OECD, 2019b).

For the economic status, four indicators were included: social spending, family benefits public spending, public spending on incapacity, and employment rate. Definition and measures of each indicators are presented below, and all data and descriptions are based on OECD data (OECD, 2019b, 2020b).

Total net social spending is defined as "public and private social expenditure including the effect of direct taxes (income tax and social security contributions), indirect taxation of consumption on cash benefits as well as tax breaks for social purposes." (OECD, 2020a). It was presented as percent of GDP as of 2015. Family benefits' public spending refers to "public spending on family benefits including financial support that is exclusively for families and children" (OECD, 2020a), and it was presented as percent of GDP as of 2015. Public spending on incapacity refers to "spending due to sickness, disability, and occupational injury," and the data was presented as percent of GDP as of 2017 or latest available data. Employment indicator was measured as the ratio of the employed to people who are aged 15–64 years old (working age population) and presented as the percent of working age population as of 2020.

For the violence/delinquency category, five indicators were included: feeling unsafe at school, victimization, smoking, drinking, and adolescents' birth. These five types of indicators have a significant linkage to one another. The indicators impact individual physical and mental health problems and cause significant damage to an entire society. As of 2016, there are 1.1 billion tobacco users aged 15 or older worldwide. Its negative impact is serious, and about half of tobacco users resulted in death. In addition, more than 80% of tobacco users are mostly from low- or middle-income countries, and vulnerable populations tend to face serious health issues than their counterparts (WHO, 2020, May 27). In addition, alcohol and smoking cause significant impairment in social and health aspects, and data shows that harmful alcohol consumption causes three million deaths every year worldwide. In addition, alcohol consumption is substantially related to crime and become a serious threat to women and children's health as well (WHO, 2018). Finally, sex-related delinquency and crime are serious problems among adolescents, and the teenage pregnancy birth rate is 44 per 1,000 adolescent girls who are 15–19 years old worldwide as of 2018. While adolescent pregnancies become a common issue globally, it is a more serious problem in countries with poverty, limited education, and lack of employment opportunities (WHO, 2020, May 27).

Each indicator in violence/delinquency category was measured as follows. Feeling unsafe at school refers to the percentage of 8th graders who disagreed and strongly disagreed with the statement "I feel safe when I am at school," and this data is based on the TIMSS 2015 survey data. Victimization is measured as the percentage of 8th graders who experienced victimization (both in- and off-online) at least once in the past year, and the data was based on the TIMSS 2015 survey data. Smoking refers to the percentage of current tobacco users aged 15 years and older as of 2015, and the data was based on WHO. Drinking refers the total alcohol per capita consumption of people who are 15 years old or older, and data includes current drinkers only as of 2016 based on the WHO database. Teenage pregnancy birth rate was measured as birth rate per 1,000 per girls 15–19 years old as of 2015, and the data was based on the WHO database.

The education category in Fig. 4.2 shows that educational spending based on percent of GDP, both public and private, is the largest in Korea compared to Japan and the U.S. Korea's public spending on education is 3.5% of GDP, while the U.S. spends 3.2% and Japan 2.5%, respectively. Korea's private spending on education is 0.5% of GDP when the U.S. spends 0.3% and Japan spends 0.2%. The economic status category shows that total net social spending including public and private social expenditure in Korea is 13%, when it is 23.5% in Japan and 30.0% in the U.S. Data of public spending on family benefits including exclusive financial support for families and children show 1.2% in Korea, when it is 1.3% in Japan and 0.6% in the U.S. Data of public spending on incapacity, such as people with sickness, disability, or occupational injury, show 0.6% in Korea, 1.0% in Japan and 1.3% in the U.S. The employment rate, one of the most frequently used indicators, is 66.7 in Korea, 78.0 in Japan, and 62.6 in the U.S.

The violence/delinquency category shows that the percent of students who feel unsafe at school is 20.0% in Korea, 28.5% and 42.9%, in Japan and the U.S., respectively. Percentage of students who are victimized is 55.2% in Korea, 59.3% in Japan, and 77.1% in the U.S. Percentage of current tobacco users aged 15 years and older is 23.1% in Korea, 21.0% in Japan and 24.9% in the U.S. Alcohol per capita consumption of current drinkers who are 15 years old or older is 10.2 in Korea, 8.0 in Japan, and 9.8 in the U.S. Finally, the birth rate for teenage pregnancies is 1.4 in Korea, 4.1 in Japan, and 22.3 in the U.S.

Summary

In this chapter, major types of crime (e.g., theft, burglary, assault, rape, robbery, and homicide) were compared in Korea, Japan, and the U.S., and national characteristics (e.g., educational and economic indicators) from each country were analyzed in relation to violence and delinquency in the three countries. While there are various national characteristics, education and economic aspects have been examined as solid linkages to violence by many researchers.

It is noticeable that portion of spending on education based on GDP is the largest in Korea among the three countries. According to the data presented in Fig. 4.2, Korea has the smaller percentages of both students who feel unsafe at school and experience victimization, compared to Japan and the U.S. Spending more in education implies the strong belief within a country to improve in educational outcomes by investing. As mentioned often throughout this book, Korean education is expressed as "education fever" or "education zeal." Korean parents are actively involved in education expecting upward social mobility for their children. Korean policymakers seek better education policies to improve academic outcomes, and multiple international tests revealed Korean students continuously outperformed in mathematics and reading subjects over the past years. Despite such outstanding outcomes, Korean education has been criticized for its extreme competition causing students' stress, anxiety, and even conflicts among peers. While Korean education environment should eradicate such negative aspects, it is important that schools should value academic achievement and encourage students to improve their outcomes. All stakeholders, including school administrators, teachers, and parents, share the same value and motivate students to focus on the right track for their future. More spending on education and sharing value on education among all stakeholders might play key roles to improve Korean students' academic and behavioral outcomes.

Percentages of smoking and drinking in the three countries show slight differences. These indicators were measured based on people who are 15 years old and older; thus, the portion of youth who smoke or drink is unclear. In future research, types of delinquency measures should be used to focus only on youth. The adolescent birth rate is the lowest in Korea, whereas the rate of the U.S. is the highest among the three countries, and it is more than 15 times greater than the Korean adolescent birth rate. Teenage pregnancy is often related to dropping out of school, drug use, violence, and other serious issues including mental health struggles. School violence should be understood and prevented with different types of problem behaviors as all problem behaviors are related one another.

This chapter briefly presents the differences of selected national indicators and youth violence in Korea, Japan, and the U.S., and limits further analysis. Although compulsory education in three countries is common (i.e., 88–93% based on OECD data), youth crime might not be the best measures of school violence. Given available international data, youth crime holds the closest data to analyze school violence. Future research needs to examine how those national indicators are linked to school violence by utilizing improved measures and analysis models. In addition, more quantified measures on discipline practices and instruction practices could be useful to explore school violence phenomenon in the three countries. Deeper insight into cultural backgrounds of Korea, Japan, and the U.S. should be included to enhance our understanding of school violence across the globe.

References

Aaron, K., & Ward, G. (2014). Race, poverty, and exclusionary school security: An empirical analysis of U.S. elementary, middle, and high schools. *Youth Violence and Juvenile Justice, 12*(4), 332–354.

Agnew, R., & White, H. R. (1992). An empirical test of general strain theory. *Criminology, 30*(4), 475–500.

Akiba, M., & Han, S. (2007). Academic differentiation, school achievement and school violence in the USA and South Korea. *Compare, 37*(2), 201–219.

Akiba, M., LeTendre, G. K., Baker, D. P., & Goesling, B. (2002). Student victimization: National and school system effects on school violence in 37 nations. *American Educational Research Journal, 39*(4), 829–853.

Akiba, M., Shimizu, K., & Zhuang, Y. (2010). Bullies, victims, teachers in Japanese middle schools. *Comparative Education Review, 54*(3), 369–392.

Avison, W. R., & Loring, P. L. (1986). Population diversity and cross-national homicide: The effects of inequality and heterogeneity. *Criminology, 24*(4), 733–749.

Baron, S. W. (2007). Street youth, gender, financial strain, and crime: Exploring Broidy and Agnew's extension to general strain theory. *Deviant Behavior, 28*(3), 273–302.

Bax, T. (2016). A contemporary history of bullying & violence in South Korean schools. *AsianCultural and History, 8*(2), 91–105.

Benbenishty, R., & Astor, R. A. (2008). School violence in an international context a call for global collaboration in research and prevention. *International Journal of Violence and Schools, 7*, 59–80.

Cho, S., & Galehan, J. (2020). Stressful life events and negative emotions on delinquency among Korean Youth: An empirical test of general strain theory assessing longitudinal mediation analysis. *International Journal of Offender Therapy and Comparative Criminology, 64*(1), 38–62.

Churchill, S. A., & Laryea, E. (2019). Crime and ethnic diversity: Cross-country evidence. *Crime & Delinquency*. Retrieved September 26, 2020, from https://doi.org/10.1177/0011128717732036

Corcoran, K. E., Pettinicchio, D., & Robbins, B. (2018). A double-edged sword: The countervailing effects of religion on cross-national violent crime. *Social Science Quarterly, 99*(1), 377–389.

Dawson, W. (2010). Private tutoring and mass schooling in East Asia: Reflections of inequality in Japan, South Korea, and Cambodia. *Asian Pacific Education Review, 11*, 14–24.

Eisner, M. (2002). Crime, problem drinking, and drug use: Patterns of problem behavior in cross-national perspective. *The Annals of the American Academy of Political and Social Science, 580*(1), 201–225.

Elgar, F. J., Craig, W., Boyce, W., Morgan, A., & Vella-Zarb, R. (2009). Income inequality and school bullying: Multilevel study of adolescents in 37 countries. *Journal of Adolescent Health, 45*, 351–359.

Felson, R. B., Osgood, D. W., Horney, J., & Wiernik, C. (2012). Having a bad month: General versus specific effects of stress on crime. *Journal of Quantitative Criminology, 28*, 347–363.

Flanagan, I. M. L., Auty, K. M., & Farrington, D. P. (2019). Parental supervision and later offending: A systematic review of longitudinal studies. *Aggression and Violent Behavior, 47*, 215–229.

Fleming, L. C., & Jacobsen, K. H. (2009). Bullying among middle-school students in low and middle income countries. *Health Promotion International, 25*(1), 73–84.

Han, S., & Akiba, M. (2011). School safety, severe disciplinary actions, and school characteristics: A secondary analysis of the school survey on crime and safety. *Journal of School Leadership, 21*(2), 262–292.

Harrendorf, S., Heiskanen, M., & Malby, S. (Eds.). (2010). *International statistics on crime and justice*. European Institute for Crime Prevention and Control, Affiliated with the United Nations (HEUNI) Publication Series No. 64. Retrieved September 26, 2020, from https://www.unodc.org/documents/data-and-analysis/Crime statistics/International_Statistics_on_Crime_and_Justice.pdf

Hsieh, C., & Pugh, M. D. (1993). Poverty, income inequality, and violent crime: A meta-analysis of recent aggregate data studies. *Criminal Justice Review, 18*(2), 182–202.

Kang, S. (2010). Democracy and human rights education in South Korea. *Journal of Comparative Education, 38*(3), 315–325.

Kim, S., & Lee, J. (2010). Private tutoring and demand for education in South Korea. *Development and Cultural Change, 58*(2), 259–296.

Kim, Y. J., Moon, S. S., Lee, J. H., & Kim, J. K. (2018). Risk factors and mediators of suicidal ideation among Korean adolescents. *Crisis, 39*, 4–12.

Kim, Y. S., Boyce, T., Koh, Y., & Leventhal, B. L. (2009). Time trends, trajectories, and demographic predictors of bullying: A prospective study in Korean adolescents. *Journal of Adolescent Health, 45*(4), 360–367.

Kwon, S. K., Lee, M., & Shin, D. (2017). Educational assessment in the Republic of Korea: lights and shadows of high-stake exam-based education system. *Assessment in Education: Principles, Policy & Practice, 24*(1), 60–77.

Lai, S., Ye, R., & Chang, U. (2008). Bullying in middle schools: An Asian-Pacific regional study. *Asia Pacific Education Review, 9*(4), 503–515.

Lane, J., & Meeker, J. W. (2000). Subcultural diversity and the fear of crime and gangs. *Crime & Delinquency, 46*(4), 497–521.

Lee, C. J., Lee, H., & Jang, H. (2010). The history of policy response to shadow education in South Korea: implications for the next cycle of policy responses. *Asia Pacific Education Review, 11*, 97–108.

Lee, E., & McDonald, J. N. (2001). Crime, delinquency, and social status: A reconstruction. *Journal of Offender Rehabilitation, 32*(3), 23–52.

Lee, J. (2001). School reform initiatives as balancing acts: Policy variation and educational convergence among Japan, Korea, England, and the United States. *Education Policy Analysis Archives, 9*(13), 1–11.

Long, A. N., & Dowdell, E. B. (2018). Online and health risk behaviors in high school students: An examination of a bullying. *Pediatric Nursing, 44*(5), 223–228.

Mason, W. A., Hitch, J. E., Kosterman, R., McCarty, C. A., Herrenkohl, T. I., & Hawkins, J. D. (2010). Growth in adolescent delinquency and alcohol use in relation to young adult crime, alcohol use disorders, and risky sex: A comparison overuse from low- versus middle-income backgrounds. *The Journal and Child Psychology and Psychiatry, 51*(12), 1377–1385.

Mednick, B., Reznick, C., Hocevar, D., & Baker, R. (1987). Long-term effects of parental divorce on young adult male crime. *Journal of Youth and Adolescence, 16*, 31–45.

Nakamura, T. (2003). Educational aspirations and the warming-up/cooling down process: A comparative study between Japan and South Korea. *Social Science Japan Journal, 6*(2), 199–220.

Nakamura, T. (2005). Educational system and parental education fever in contemporary Japan: Comparison with the case of South Korea. *KEDI Journal of Educational Policy, 2*(1), 35–50.

Poushter, J., & Fetterolf, J. (2019, April 22). *A change world: Global views on diversity, gender equality, family life and the importance of religion.* Pew Research Center. Retrieved September 26, 2020, from https://www.pewresearch.org/global/2019/04/22/how-people-around-the-world-view-diversity-in-their-countries/

Pratt, T. C., & Lowenkamp, C. T. (2002). Conflict theory, economic conditions and homicide: A time-series analysis. *Homicide Studies, 6*(1), 61–83.

Rosenfeld, R. (2009). Crime is the problem: Homicide, acquisitive crime, and economic conditions. *Journal of Quantitative Criminology, 25*, 287–306.

Seth, M. (2012). Education zeal, state control and citizenship in South Korea. *Citizenship Studies, 16*(1), 13–28.

Shin, S., & Koh, M. (2005). Korean education in cultural context. *Essays in Education, 14*(10). https://openriver.winona.edu/eie/vol14/iss1/10

Sirvanli-Ozen, D. (2008). Impact of divorce on the behavior and adjustment problems, parenting styles, and attachment styles of children. *Journal of Divorce & Marriage, 42*(3–4), 127–151.

Skiba, R. J., Michael, R. S., Nardo, A. C., & Peterson, R. L. (2002). The color of discipline: Sources of racial and gender disproportionality in school punishment. *Urban Review, 34*(4), 317–342.

Soysa, I., & Noel, C. (2020). Does ethnic diversity increase violent crime? A global analysis of homicide rates 1995–2013. *European Journal of Criminology, 17*(2), 175–198.

United Nations Office on Drugs and Crime. (2018). *UNODC data portal.* Retrieved September 26, 2020, from https://dataunodc.un.org/

Wadsworth, T. (2010). Is immigration responsible for the crime drop? An assessment of the influence of immigration on changes in violent crime between 1990 and 2000. *Social Science Quarterly, 91*(2), 531–553.

Weaver, J. M., & Schofield, T. J. (2015). Mediation and moderation of divorce effects on children's behavior problems. *Journal of Family Psychology, 29*(1), 39–48.

Welsh, R. O., & Little, S. (2018). The school discipline dilemma: A comprehensive review of disparities and alternative approaches. *Review of Educational Research, 88*(5), 752–794.

Data Sources

OECD. (2011). *Doing better for families.* Retrieved September 26, 2020, from https://www.oecd.org/els/soc/47701118.pdf

OECD. (2017). *PISA 2015 results (Volume III): students' well-being.* OECD Publishing. Retrieved September 26, 2020, from http://dx.doi.org/10.1787/9789264273856-en

OECD. (2018a). *PISA 2015 results in focus.* Retrieved September 26, 2020, from https://www.oecd.org/pisa/pisa-2015-results-in-focus.pdf

OECD. (2018b). *Education policy in Japan: Building bridges towards 2030.* Reviews of National Policies for Education. Retrieved September 26, 2020, from https://doi.org/10.1787/9789264302402-en

OECD. (2019a).*International migration outlook 2019.* OECD Publishing. Retrieved September 26, 2020, from https://doi.org/10.1787/c3e35eec-en

OECD. (2019b). *Government at a glance.* Retrieved August 26, 2020, from https://www.oecd.org

OECD. (2019c). *PISA 2018 results (Volume II): Where all students can succeed.* OECD Publishing. Retrieved September 26, 2020, from https://doi.org/10.1787/b5fd1b8f-en

OECD. (2020a). *National population distribution (indicator).* https://doi.org/10.1787/7314f74f-en. Accessed on September 26, 2020.

OECD. (2020b). *Employment rate, young population, and the structure of family.* Retrieved September 26, 2020 from https://data.oecd.org/

World Health Organization. (2018). *Global status report on alcohol and health 2018.* World Health Organization. License: CC BY-NC-SA 3.0 IGO. Retrieved September 26, 2020, from https://apps.who.int/iris/bitstream/handle/10665/274603/9789241565639-eng.pdf?ua=1

World Health Organization. (2019). *WHO global report on trends in prevalence of tobacco smoking 2000–2025* (2nd ed.). World Health Organization. Retrieved September 26, 2020, from https://apps.who.int/iris/bitstream/handle/10665/272694/9789241514170-eng.pdf?ua=1

World Health Organization. (2020, May 27). *Key facts: Tobacco, alcohol, and adolescent pregnancy.* Retrieved September 26, 2020, from https://www.who.int/news-room/fact-sheets

Chapter 5
School Characteristics and School Violence

School violence prevention has been discussed from many different perspectives, yet there is an agreement that school violence is prevented not by one factor but multiple factors with the multilevel prevention strategies (Centers for Disease Control and Prevention, 2017; Johnson et al., 2017; Larsen, 2003; Webster & Champion, 1993). School administrators, teachers, students, parents, and the community should cooperate with one another to achieve school safety. Predictors of school violence have been extensively investigated by many researchers around the world, and school characteristics are an important context to capture predictors of school violence. While there are differences in school system, culture, and value across nations, some school characteristics are universally known as strong predictors of school violence.

This chapter presents school characteristics that are related to school violence in Korea, Japan, and the U.S. School characteristics for the analysis are composed of school location, school poverty, teacher factor, parent factor, and student factor. These indicators are from principals' report in the TIMSS 2015 survey data. Principals were given five types of school location: (1) urban-densely populated, (2) suburban-on fringe or outskirts of urban area, (3) medium-size city or large town, (4) small town or village, and (5) remote rural. Poverty was measured by the principals' report of percentage of students who are from economically disadvantaged homes. The teacher factor was assessed by two items: (1) ability to inspire students and (2) expectations for students' academic achievement. The parent factor was measured by four items including parents': (1) ensuring students' learning readiness, (2) expectation of students' academic achievement, (3) emphasizing high academic standard, and (4) support for academic achievement. The student factor was measured by two items: (1) motivated to do well in school and (2) respect peer's outperformance. Finally, school violence is measured by the principals' report indicating whether or not a violent incident is problematic. Six types of violence types were given: (1) profanity, (2) vandalism, (3) intimidation among students, (4) physical injury to students, (5) intimidation of teachers, and (6) physical injury to teachers.

© Springer Nature Singapore Pte Ltd. 2021
S. Han, *School Violence in South Korea*,
https://doi.org/10.1007/978-981-16-2730-9_5

School Characteristics and School Violence in Literature

Researchers found indicators of school violence from multiple levels, such as individual student background, teachers' attitudes and perspectives, parental involvement, school context including location, school size, poverty, academic achievement, racial proportion in student population, residential mobility, and social disorganization (Akiba & Han, 2007; Cantor & Wright, 2001; Han 2014; Han & Akiba, 2011; Shuval et al., 2012).

To compare school characteristics and school violence in Korea, Japan, and the U.S., previous studies on school location (urban), poverty, teacher's roles and perspectives, parental involvement, and students' outcomes were reviewed from the literature.

Many empirical studies examined school violence with context factors, such as urbanicity and poverty. Urbanization is a global phenomenon, and more than 4 billion people live in urban areas, which is more people than in rural areas around the world. While urbanization is expanded, poverty becomes a critical issue. Nearly 1 in 3 people in urban areas live in slum households that lack access to improved water and sanitation, proper living area, and endurance of housing (Ritchie & Roser, 2019). Since schools are influenced by neighborhoods, urbanicity and poverty need to be understood as context to predict school violence.

Urbanicity and poverty. Urban area as a school location has been examined as one of the predictors of school violence. A large number of studies have demonstrated that urban schools tend to experience more violence than other areas. A national sample of U.S. schools showed a higher rate of student victimization in urban schools than other areas. Rates of victimization by theft and violent incident per 1,000 students ages 12–18 reveal 49.5 in urban and 29.0 in rural. A total of 377,400 students were victimized by such incidents in urban areas in 2017. In the same year, 8.6% of students reported gang presence in school nationwide. Urban students notice such gang presence in school nearly two times more than their counterparts in rural areas; 11.3% of students ages 12–18 reported gang presence in urban schools and 6.6% of students reported such incidents in rural schools. For the 2015–2016 school year, 33.9% of public schools in urban areas reported 72,300 violent incidents to police, whereas 25.9% of public schools in rural areas reported 29,700 violent incidents to police. In the same school year, nearly half of the teaching staff at urban schools (49.6%) reported that students' misbehaviors interfered with their teaching, whereas only 37.1% of their counterparts in rural schools reported such incidents (Musu, Zhang, Wang, Zhang, & Oudeker, 2019).

In urbanization, poverty is another element to be discussed. Poverty is one of the strongest factors linking to violence in literature (Akiba, LeTendre, Baker, & Goesling, 2002; Jansen, Veenstra, Ormel, Verhulst, & Reijneveld, 2011; Kim, Lee, Jung, Jaime, & Cubbin, 2019; Rekker et al., 2015; Ullery, Gonzalez, & Katz, 2016). Poverty causes a lack of social support and social control that are needed to prevent crime (Kramer, 2010). Extensive meta-analysis of 34 aggregate data studies on the relationship between poverty and crime showed that poverty and income inequality are associated with violent crime, such as homicide and assault (Hsieh & Pugh, 1993). Many researchers found such relationships with different measures of poverty. Some researchers assess the level of community poverty based on amount of welfare dependency, poverty, substance abuse, and crime (Ullery et al., 2016) and gross domestic product at the national level (Akiba et al., 2002). Most commonly, school poverty is measured by percentage of students' lunch status (e.g., eligibility for free and/or reduced-price lunch) or parents' educational level, occupation, and income level.

Literature shows how poverty is related to school violence and impacts school safety. A study based on data of 37 nations showed that gross domestic product (GDP) per capita is significantly associated with national rates of school violence after controlling for school characteristics. GDP is commonly used by researchers to measure national economic status, and this study concludes that nations with a high GDP per capita are less likely to have school violence measured by student and peer victimization (Akiba et al., 2002).

Children who have parents with lower socioeconomic status are more likely to involve themselves in bullying behavior as both offender or victim (Jansen et al., 2011); bullies are also more likely to have lower socioeconomic status (SES). Survey results of approximately 3,000 middle school students in Japan showed that bullies are more likely to have less educated parents and less educational resources at home (Akiba, Shimizu, & Zhuang, 2010). Data of 503 boys from the cohort of the Pittsburgh Youth Study showed that parents' SES influences a boy's delinquent behavior over the years. Parents' SES was assessed by parents' education level, occupation, household income, and status of having welfare. Boys' behaviors were measured by statements from the mother (primary caretaker), convictions, and self-reports. Data of ten consecutive years with boys aged 7–18 shows that boys tend to commit delinquent behaviors during years when their parents' SES is lower than the years when their parents' SES is higher (Rekker et al., 2015).

While research demonstrates poverty and crime to have serious and negative impact on children, the impact can be reduced by employing an early intervention program. Data from 54 students who live in high crime and poverty areas was analyzed to examine prenatal drugs exposure and developmental delays. Results revealed that students who participated in center-based modality show significantly higher scores in reading and math than students who participated in the home-based learning modality (Ullery et al., 2016).

A longitudinal study explored that a poor neighborhood, measured by the federal poverty category in a census tract, is negatively associated with social cohesion and safety. This association is observed only among children who experienced long-term family poverty when they were 3–5 years old. Participating mothers who live in poor neighborhood are less likely to perceive that people help their neighbors and are more likely to observe drug dealers, drunks, or gang activity in the neighborhood. This association causes more externalizing problems (e.g., destruction, disobedience, and other behavioral problems) among their children in high-poverty neighborhood than their counterparts in low-poverty neighborhood (Kim et al., 2019).

A study shows that poverty has a significant impact on youth problem behaviors. Data from 489 youth who were between the ages 14 and 16 who experienced being detained in the juvenile justice system was analyzed to examine how social context influences their behaviors. Youth's social context was measured by whether they live in subsidized housing, receive free school lunch, and if they witness crime in their neighborhood. Results show that there are no significant correlations among social context, age, gender, and race/ethnicity, yet social context is significantly correlated with being involved in gang activity, knowing gang members, and committing sexually risky behaviors. Lack of social context is significantly associated with being involved in such problem behaviors, even after controlling for familial and social support and being enrolled in school (Voison et al., 2017). A qualitative study based on data of 45 students (4th, 5th, and 8th grades) revealed multilevel predictors of violence. Unequal socioeconomic status in communities, absence of parents in the household, having crime and gang activities in neighborhoods, and lack of anger management skills are found as major risk factors (Shuval et al., 2012). Poverty in rural areas also links to a youth's exposure to violence. Data from 476 youth reveals that a high-poverty community, assessed by the percentage of free and reduced-price lunch, is more likely to be related to a higher level of exposure to violence, such as threats, beating, violence involving a knife or gun, and sexual abuse (Carlson, 2006).

While many studies pointed out poverty, economic inequality, and unstable parents' SES as strong predictors of school violence, being affluent is also related to certain types of violence. Coley, Sims, Dearing, and Spielvogel (2018) analyzed data of 13,179 high school students from 76 school to see the patterns of risk behaviors among students. Results showed that students in affluent schools are more likely to be involved in property crime or drug use, whereas students in poorer schools are more likely to be involved in interpersonal violence, such as fighting or using a weapon. In addition, family or community income showed less predictive link to youth risk behaviors (Coley et al., 2018).

Teachers' support. Student victimization could be prevented by adult's monitoring and intervening, like by teachers who spend a lot of time and interact with students at school. Teachers are the ones who would notice student misbehaviors at school and could help victimized students. Thus, a teacher's perception on bullying problem is important and should be the first stage for developing bullying prevention policies (Dake, Price, Telljohann, & Funk, 2003; Organisation for Economic Co-operation and Development, 2018; Wang, Swearer, Lembeck, Collins, & Berry, 2015). Empirical studies have demonstrated the teacher's role as one of the most effective intervening factors for preventing school violence. Data from 435 middle school students revealed that more 6th graders than 7th graders tend to have more positive relationship with teachers, and bully group and bully and victims group tend to have poor relationships with their teachers. Students who have a positive relationship with teachers and strong bonds with them are likely to result in less bullying behaviors. This relationship was explained that students are less likely to be involved in bullying because teachers influence students to internalize their teacher's negative attitude toward bullying behavior (Wang, et al., 2015).

Survey results based on the data of 318 middle school students in Korea revealed that students who trust their teachers are more likely to improve in their school performance. This study emphasized middle school students might be more independent in instruction structure compared to elementary school students, and building a trusting relationship with teachers is essential for students to improve academic achievement, motivation, and adjustment (Lee, 2007). Another study in the Korean context showed that schools where teachers stress the importance of students' understanding are more likely to have a lower level of fear of being victimized by school violence (Akiba & Han, 2007). An empirical study based on a dataset of Japanese middle school students explored how students who bully peers by excluding from the group are more likely to have a weak bond with their teacher and perceive a lack of instructional support from teachers (Akiba et al., 2010).

It is worthy to note differences in teachers' role in Korea, Japan, and the U.S. More independent instruction structure/schedule and having homeroom teachers could be one of the most distinguishing features among the three nations. In the U.S., students from middle schools have no homeroom teachers and are more independent compared to their counterparts in Korea and Japan. Students in Korea and Japan have homeroom teachers until high school, and they are more likely to take classes as a whole group on the same class schedule. Homeroom teachers in Korea and Japan deal with students' every aspect including academic achievement, behavior management and counselling. Thus, the relationship between teachers and students is a vital factor for student success (Akiba et al., 2010; Ellington, 2005; Lee, 2007). Despite such different expectations and roles of teachers among the three countries, teachers in all three countries have a significant influence over students both academically and behaviorally. An international study shows that schools with teachers treating students in a fair manner are less likely to have bullying incidents (Organisation for Economic Co-operation and Development, 2018).

Parental involvement and student outcomes. Parents play a vital role in improving students' outcomes academically and behaviorally. Studies showed that parents' being involved in school discipline policies, monitoring their child's peer relationships, and using high-quality communication skills with their child significantly impact the child's behaviors and promotes their success as a student (Liu, Wong, & Roland, 2018; Low & Espelage, 2014; Xin, 2001).

An extensive meta-analysis on parenting and peer victimization studies published between 1970 and 2012 found that positive parenting, such as quality communication between child and parents, parental supervision, and affectionate relationship between students and parents, tends to be a protective factor for victimization. In addition, bullies and bully/victims tend to have experience being abused and neglected by their parents (Lereya, Samara, & Wolke, 2013).

A study based on the data from 652 students transitioning from middle to high schools in urban area of the U.S. showed that parental control has a strong impact on student's outcomes. When students have more parental control, those students are more likely to have academic motivation and less likely to have violent behaviors (Frey, Ruchkin, Martin, & Schwab-Stone, 2009). To reduce victimization, support from both parents and the community is essential. Data from 421 urban schools in the

U.S. revealed that schools that receive more support from parents and communities are less likely to have student problem behaviors. Schools with high level of parental involvement in training programs about school discipline and a formal process about school crime or discipline policies are less likely to have students' problem behaviors at the elementary school level. In addition, when a school makes a cooperative effort to promote a safer school environment with the involvement of multiple community agencies, such as social service agencies, mental health agencies, religious organizations, or juvenile justice agencies, those schools are less likely to have students' problem behaviors at the high school level (Han, 2010). Notably, the impact of parental support on students' outcomes could differ by mother and father. Survey data from 205 ethnic minority middle school students in urban areas in the U.S. showed that a mother's warmer parenting style positively influences the relationship between students' school engagement and motivation, whereas a father's warmer parenting style significantly influences the negative relationship between students' school trouble and monitoring (Lowe & Dotterer, 2013). Researchers found the differences of parenting styles by offenders and victims. Data of 205 students and their parents in an ethnically diverse urban school district in the U.S. showed that both of bullies and victims tend to have parents who mistreat their children. While victims are more likely to have parents who criticize and have less rules, bullies are more likely to have parents who supervise less and expose their children to domestic violence (Holt, Kantor, & Finkelhor, 2008).

Influences of parental support and involvement in students' outcomes have been demonstrated in multiple regions. More than 13,000 middle school students in North Africa revealed that parents' supervision is an influential factor that could reduce victimization. Students in Egypt, Morocco and Tunisia are less likely to involve peer victimization when they are subject to their parents' monitoring (e.g., parents who check child's homework and know how the child spent free time) (Abdirahman, Fleming, & Jacobsen, 2013). Another study on parental factors and bullying behaviors in Turkey showed that the lack of parental support (e.g., encouraging the child to do well, having an interest in what happened at school, and helping the child with homework) and particularly the lack of a father's supervision (e.g., knowing child's friends and child's whereabouts after school) are significantly associated with both bullying behaviors and victimization (Ethem Erginoz et al., 2013). Data of 4,855 Finnish youth ages 15–16 showed that how parents' monitoring and parents' relationship are associated to youth's hate crime. Students were asked whether their parents know where their child is after school, follow up on their grades, or ask who they get along as well as witness parents' fight. Among the participating youth, 22 percent reported being involved in bullying or assault in the past 12 months and 2.3% of youth committed hate crime. Youth who lack their parents' supervision and frequently witness parent's fight are more likely to be involved in hate crimes (Näsi, Aaltonen, & Kivivuori, 2016).

Considering the positive impacts of parental involvement and different parenting styles on students, it is important for both schools and parents to cooperate in developing antibullying policies due to the variety in parenting styles and perspective on bullying behaviors (Georgiou, 2010; Liu et al., 2018). Data of 252 elementary school students and their mothers showed that an overprotective parenting style is more likely to increase likelihood of being victimized (Georgiou, 2010), and survey studies revealed that some parents encourage their child to fight back an offender while ignoring their child's current state of victimization (Johnson, Waasdorp, Gaias, & Bradshaw, 2019) or are unaware that their child is the offender (Holt et al., 2008).

Empirical studies have demonstrated the relationship between victimization, students' academic achievement, attitude, and motivation (Akiba & Han, 2007; Cho & Choi, 2017; Klein, 2012; Ladd, Ettekal, & Lochenderfer-Ladd, 2017; Milam, Furr-Holden, & Leaf, 2010). A longitudinal study in Korea showed that physical and relational bullying contribute to a decrease in standardized test scores in Korean language, English, and mathematics. Data from more than 3,200 students in Seoul reveals that students who were verbally bullied are less likely to have a significant decrease on their test scores compared to students who were not bullied. However, students who were victimized physically and relationally are more likely to have lower scores on standardized tests anyway (Cho & Choi, 2017). Being exposed to neighborhood crime has a negative impact on student's math and reading achievement and perceived safety increases the achievement (Milam et al., 2010), and low-achieving schools are more likely to have school violence incident in the U. S. (Akiba & Han, 2007).

Student's motivation, attitude toward academic achievement, and school engagement are significant predictors for school success and the levels of such characteristics differ by students. A study, based on data from 383 K-12 students, showed that students who are often victimized (high-chronic victimization) tend to have lower levels of academic achievement, school engagement, and academic self-perceptions (Ladd et al., 2017). Data from 1895 6th grade students showed that perceived self-efficacy mediates the relationship between victimization and academic achievement. Students who were victimized tend to have lower academic achievement, and it is because they perceive they have lower self-efficacy (Thijs & Verkuyten, 2008). Such negative impact of victimization in the present or past continues to adulthood. Data of 130 students showed that students who experienced victimization in the past or are currently being victimized have a significantly lower level of motivation than students who do not have such experiences. Those victimized students are less likely to have competence and autonomy and more likely to have challenges in academic achievement, even without present victimization in college (Young-Jones, Fursa, Byrket, & Sly, 2015).

Comparison of School Characteristics and School Violence in Korea, Japan, and the U.S.

School principals' survey results from the TIMSS datasets were analyzed to compare school characteristics and school violence. Data analysis with each variable's description is presented as follows.

Data and Analysis

From the TIMSS survey data, school principals' survey data was used; the sample size was as follows: 150 in Korea, 147 in Japan, and 220 in the U.S. School characteristics were included as urbanicity, percentage of students from economically disadvantaged families, and factors of teachers, parents, and students.

Urbanicity was assessed by asking principals "which best describes the immediate area in which your school is located?" Principals responded to one out of five choices: urban-densely populated, suburban-on fringe or outskirts of urban area, medium-size city or large town, small town, or village and remote rural.

Poverty was assessed by the percentage of students from economically disadvantaged households. Principals were asked "approximately what percentage of students in your school have the following background-come from economically disadvantaged homes?" Principals responded to one out of four choices: 0–10%, 11–25%, 26–50%, and more than 50%.

Three school factors were included in the analysis. First, the teacher factor was measured with two items. Principals assessed their teachers by either, (1) teachers have ability to inspire students, and (2) teachers expect students' academic achievement. Second, principals assessed parents using four items: (1) parents ensure students' learning readiness, (2) parents expect students' academic achievement, (3) parents stress maintaining high academic standard, and 4) parents support for students' academic achievement. Finally, students' factor was assessed using two items. Principals assessed (1) students want to do well in school, and (2) students respect classmates' outperformance in academic achievement. Principals assessed those items regarding teachers, parents and student factors based on a scale ranging from 1 (very high) to 5 (very low). In the analysis, those variables were reverse-coded. The mean of the two items of the teacher factor, the four items of the parent factor, and the two items of the student factor were computed, respectively, and created indexes for each teacher, parent, and student factor. Reliability of each index is as follows: teacher factor (Cronbach's alpha $= 0.744$), parent factor (Cronbach's alpha $= 0.875$), and student factor (Cronbach's alpha $= 0.698$).

School violence was assessed based on principals' reports. Originally, principals were asked to assess multiple forms of violent behaviors in school and responded to 1 (not a problem), 2 (minor problem), 3 (moderate problem), and 4 (serious problem).

For the analyses, six forms of school violence including profanity, vandalism, intimidation among students, physical injury to students, intimidation of teachers, and physical injury to teachers were used.

Included in the descriptive statistics were schools that were reported as having no problem in the six forms of school violence and schools that were reported having minor to serious problem in school violence.

Results

School principals reported the percentage of students from economically disadvantaged families. As Fig. 5.1 shows, more than 40% of Japanese schools, less than 30% of Korean schools, and about 15% of U.S. schools have less than 10% of students from economically disadvantaged families. Approximately 42% of Japanese schools and 35% of Korean schools were reported to have 11–25% of students from economically disadvantaged families, whereas 14% of U.S. schools reported those students. Interestingly, more than 43% of U.S. schools reported more than half of students as from economically disadvantaged family, whereas only 10.7% of Korean schools and 1.4% of Japanese schools reported those students.

It is common that "economically disadvantaged students" are identified whether they are eligible for free and/or reduced-price lunch in public schools, yet this question in the TIMSS may ask for a more generic observation rather than the school lunch status. The TIMSS survey also provides data about the percentage of students who are eligible for free breakfast and lunch. However, this question does not necessarily measure poverty in the international context and should be understood with each nations' unique school lunch policies. For example, in Korea, 70.7% of public schools serve free lunch to all students (based on the TIMSS 2015 data analyses). Since 2011, with an ongoing debate on free school lunch policy, Korean public

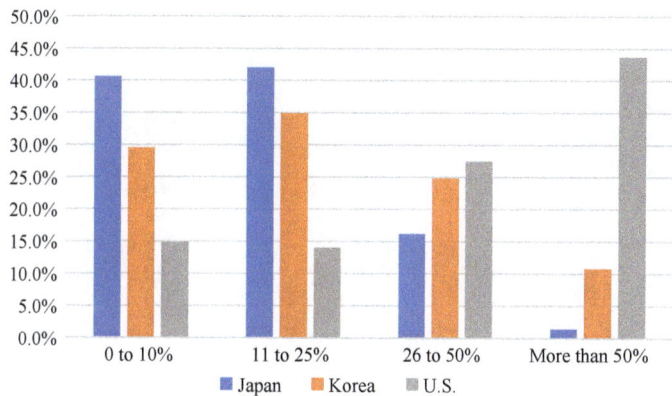

Fig. 5.1 Percentage of students from economically disadvantaged families

schools attempt to provide free lunch to all students regardless of their economic status (Choe, 2011; Schuman, 2011). About 15% of U.S. public schools and less than 3% of Japanese schools provide free meals to all students. Assessing poverty based on the percentage of students receiving free meals at school should be used with caution in research on the international level.

Figure 5.2 shows the percentage of the type of area where schools are located. More than 36% of Korean schools are in urban areas, and about half of Japanese schools are in either medium sized city or large towns. Compared to Korea and Japan, the U. S. schools are spread out across various types of areas. About 30% of U.S. schools are in the suburbs, 23.8% of schools are in medium sized cities or large towns, 22.4% of schools are in urban areas, 18.8% of schools are in small towns, and 5.8% of schools are in rural areas.

Figure 5.3 presents school characteristics regarding teacher, parent, and student factors. Overall, Korean schools show a higher level of each factor than those of Japanese and U.S. schools. On average, Korean principals report that teachers who

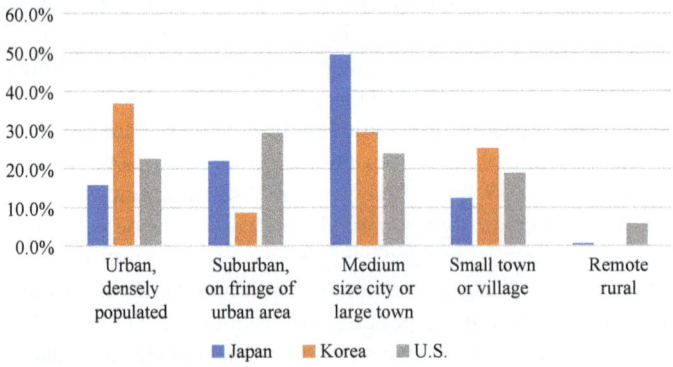

Fig. 5.2 Percentage of school by location

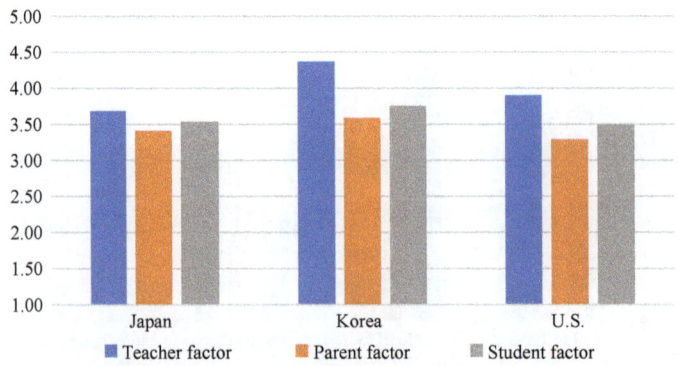

Fig. 5.3 Comparison of school characteristics. *Note* Scales range from 1 (very low) to 5 (very high)

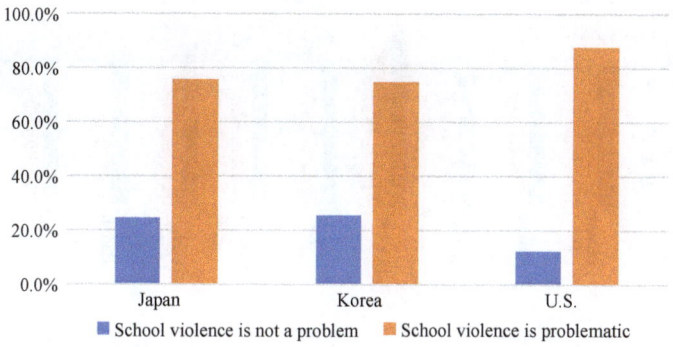

Fig. 5.4 Percentage of schools with problematic violence incidents

inspire and expect higher academic achievement for their students (4.37) when the level of teacher factor is at 3.69 and 3.90 in the U.S. and Japan, respectively. Korean school principals report that parents ensure students' learning readiness, expect students' achievement, stress maintaining high academic standard, and support for students' academic achievement (3.59) when the level of parent factor is at 3.41 and 3.29 in Japan and the U.S., respectively. Korean school principals report that students try to do well in school and respect their classmate's outperformance (3.76) when the level of the student factor is at 3.53 and 3.49 in Japan and the U.S., respectively. While parent and student factors show a similar level across nations, the teacher factor in Korea is noticeably higher than that of Japan and the U.S.

As Fig. 5.4 shows, when comparing school violence is computed for the sum of the six forms of school violence, 25.3% of Korean schools, 24.5% of Japanese schools, and 12.3% of U.S. schools reported school violence as not a problem in school. Principals from the rest of the schools reported at least one of the six forms of school violence being problematic in school.

Figure 5.5 shows the comparison of school characteristics by level of school violence. The level of school violence is measured whether school principals report violence as not a problem or more than four forms of violence are problematic.

Regarding teacher factors, principals in schools with lower level of violence more positively assessed teachers' ability to inspire students' academic achievement and teacher's expectation for student achievement than those in schools with a higher level of violence (4.63 vs. 4.27 in Korea, 3.92 vs. 3.36 in Japan, and 4.37 vs. 3.62 in the U.S.). Literature shows a teacher's vital role in decreasing bullying incidents. Teachers with high expectation for students tend to give more feedback to students and handle students' behavior in a more positive manner (Rubie-Davies, 2007), and student's perceived teacher efficacy in reducing bullying incidents is more likely to decrease peer-reported bullying incidents (Veenstra, Lindenberg, Huitsing, Sainio, & Salmivalli, 2014). Regarding parent factors, principals in schools with a lower level of violence more positively assessed that parents' active involvement in students' academic achievement than those in schools with a higher level of violence. Parents in schools with a lower level of violence ensure students' learning readiness, support

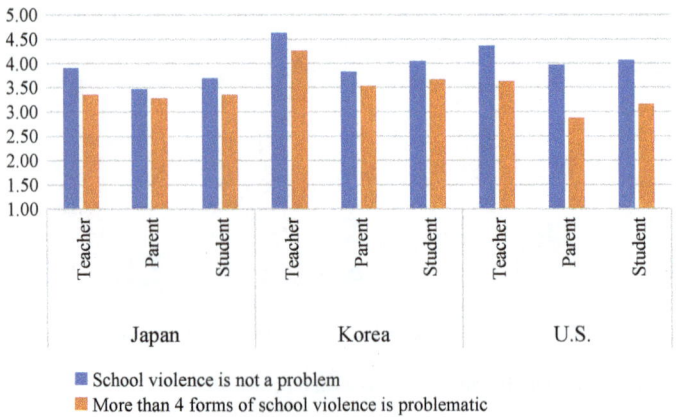

Fig. 5.5 School characteristics and school violence. *Note* Scales ranged from 1 (very low) to 5 (very high); sample size is Japan = 75, Korea = 90, and U.S. = 108

and have higher expectation for students' academic achievement, and stress meeting and maintaining a high academic standard (3.84 vs.3.54 in Korea, 3.47 vs. 3.28 in Japan, and 3.97 vs.2.87 in the U.S.). Regarding student factors, principals in schools with a lower level of violence assessed students' attitudes more positively than those in schools with a higher level of violence. That is, students in schools with less violence are more likely to have the desire to do well in school and respect their classmate's outperformance than those in schools with more violence (4.05 vs.3.66 in Korea, 3.69 vs.3.36 in Japan, and 4.07 vs. 3.16 in U.S.).

While the patterns shown in the teacher, parent, and student factors between schools with less and more violence are consistent across the three nations, there are several distinguishing features.

First, on average, the teacher, parent, and student factors in Japan were assessed as the lowest by principals in comparison to Korea and the U.S. All three factors assessed below 4 on a scale of 5 (results ranged from 3.92 to 3.28).

Second, Korean teacher factors are assessed as the highest regardless of school violence in comparison to reports from Japanese and U.S. teachers. Korean teachers assessed 4.63 and 4.27, whereas Japanese teachers assessed 3.92 and 3.36 and U.S. teachers assessed 4.37 and 3.62. In Korea, teachers are highly respected in society and the public respect for teachers in Korea was globally recognized when it ranked fourth among the OECD member nations (Oh, 2013). Teaching has been one of the most popular occupations among the younger generation in Korea because of employee benefits, such as stability, competitive pay, and good work environment in addition to the respected social standing (Center on International Education Benchmark, 2018). Thus, to obtain a teaching certificate is competitive, which helps select the most highly qualified teachers as well as continue improving teacher quality. Although Korean teachers are more positively assessed in schools with less violence than schools with more violence, teachers in both schools are assessed highly (on average, 4.63 and 4.27 out of 5, respectively).

Third, the gap between schools with a lower level of violence and schools with a higher level of violence is greater in U.S. schools than Japanese and Korean schools. In the U.S., safer schools are more likely to have teachers' inspiration and expectations for student academic achievement, active parental involvement and students' motivation toward academic achievement and value peers' outperformance than schools with more violence. Particularly parental involvement in U.S. schools with more violence is assessed as the lowest (2.87) among the three factors across the three nations. There is a significantly large gap between parental involvement in U.S. schools with a lower and higher level of violence (3.97 vs. 2.87) than Japanese (3.47 vs. 3.36) and Korean schools (3.84 vs. 3.54). While it is well known that school violence is more common where parents are less supportive and less involved in students' academic achievement, this is more noticeable in U.S. schools than in Korea and Japan.

Summary

In this chapter, school characteristics in Korea, Japan, and the U.S. were examined to see how school characteristics differ by level of school violence. First, poverty and school location were examined on how they impact school characteristics across nations. Poverty was measured by principals' report of the percentage of students who come from economically disadvantaged families among the five types of school locations (from urban to rural) for principals to select in the survey. Teachers' inspiration to students and expectation for their academic achievement, parents' support and involvement in students' academic achievement, and student's attitude toward academic performance were compared by level of school violence. In addition, a multiple regression analysis was conducted to see how teacher, parent, and student factors are related to school contextual factors.

Based on report of public school principals on poverty, 10.7% of Korean schools reported having more than 50% of students come from economically disadvantaged families, while Japanese schools and U.S. schools reported only 1.4% and 43%, respectively. On the other hand, about 30% of Korean schools have less than 10% of students from economically disadvantaged students, whereas it was reported as 40% for Japanese schools and 15% for U.S. schools.

The largest percentage of Korean schools (36.7%) are located in urban areas, whereas the largest percent of Japanese schools (49.3%) are located in medium-size cities or large towns and 29.1% of U.S. schools are located in suburban areas. Compared to Korean schools, public schools in Japan and the U.S. are less likely to be in urban areas; 15.8% of Japanese schools and 22.4% of U.S. schools are located in urban areas. In addition, U.S. public schools are more likely to be spread out across various locations than Korean public schools and Japanese public schools (about 30% of U.S. schools are in the suburbs, 23.8% in medium size cities or large towns, 22.4% in urban areas, and 18.8% in small towns and 5.8% in rural areas).

Three factors measured by teachers' inspiration to students and expectation of their academic achievement, parents' support and involvement in students' academic achievement, and student's attitude toward academic performance revealed higher levels in Korea than Japan and the U.S. Public school principals in Korea assessed teachers' inspiration to students and having expectations for students as 4.37 based on a scale of 1 (very low) to 5 (very high). Their counterparts reported under four points: 3.69 in Japan and 3.90 in the U.S. The parental factor measured by their support and involvement for students' academic performance and Korean principals' assessment is higher than that of Japan and the U.S. Korean principals assessed parental support and involvement as 3.59, whereas Japanese principals and U.S. principals reported as 3.41 and 3.29, respectively. The student factor measured students' positive attitude toward academic performance and recognition of peers' outperformance as higher than that of Japan and the U.S. Korean principals assessed student's positive attitude as 3.76, whereas it was assessed as 3.53 in Japan and 3.49 in the U.S.

Overall, principals' reports on parent and student factors reveal similar levels across the three nations with numbers being just slightly higher in Korea. However, it is noticeable that Korean teachers are highly recognized by principals in terms of their ability to inspire and have high expectations for their students than their counterparts in Japan and the U.S.

Public school principals reported whether their schools have a violence problem or not and were given six forms of school violence to reference (profanity, vandalism, intimidation and verbal abuse, physical injury, violence toward teachers including intimidation, and physical injury).

About a quarter of Korean and Japanese public schools reported having no problems of school violence (25.3% and 24.5%, respectively) and 12.3% of U.S. principals reported that they do have a school violence problem. The rest of the principals perceived their school violence problem as minor, moderate, or serious (74.7% in Korea, 75.5% in Japan, and 87.7% in the U.S., respectively).

A comparison of teacher, parent, and student factors with school violence consistently showed that schools with a higher report of those factors are less likely to have school violence. Schools having teachers who inspire students and have high expectations for their students' academic performance are less likely to have school violence problems. The teacher factor was 4.63 in schools with a lower school violence vs. 4.27 in schools with a higher level of school violence in Korea, 3.92 vs. 3.36 in Japan, and 4.37 vs. 3.62 in the U.S., respectively. As shown, the different levels of the teacher factor between schools with a lower and a higher level of school violence are larger in the U.S. than Korea and Japan as supported by literature. Teachers' expectation for students and teacher efficacy in reducing bullying both have a positive influence on discipline practices and decrease peer-reported bullying incidents; the presence of those elements tends to discipline student's behaviors in a positive manner (Rubie-Davies, 2007; Veenstra, et al., 2014).

Schools with a higher level of parental involvement tend to have a lower level of school violence. In Korea, parental factor was assessed as 3.84 in schools with a lower level of school violence and 3.54 in schools with a higher level of school violence, 3.47 and 3.28 in Japan, and 3.97 and .2.87 in the U.S., respectively. While U.S. schools have the highest points of parental factor in school with a lower level of school violence among the three nations, U.S. schools also have the lowest points of parental factor in schools with high school violence. Among the three nations, U.S. schools have a larger difference in the level of parental involvement between schools with lower and higher school violence.

The countries whose school principals reported a higher level in students' positive attitude tend to have a lower level of violence; students are more likely to have the desire to do well in school performance and respect their peers' achievement in schools, which is paired with a lower level of violence. Levels of students' positive attitude toward academic outcomes are 4.05 in schools with lower school violence and 3.66 in schools with a higher level of school violence in Korea, 3.69 vs. 3.36 in Japan, and 4.07 vs. 3.16 in the U.S., respectively.

As presented above, the patterns of schools with high levels of the teacher, parent, and student factors and a lower level of school violence are observed. Yet, there are different patterns in each of the three nations. On average, Japanese schools were assessed with the lowest numbers in all three factors based on the principals' report. All factors in Japanese schools revealed below four points on a scale of five, ranging from just 3.92 to 3.28.

Regardless of the level of school violence, teacher factors in Korea reveal the highest points among the three nations. Korean teachers are assessed as 4.63 in schools with low school violence and 4.27 in schools with high school violence, whereas Japanese teachers are assessed as 3.92 and 3.36, and U.S. teachers are assessed as 4.37 and 3.62.

In Korea, teaching professions are traditionally highly respected by society; even today, teaching professions have been one of the most popular occupations among the younger generation. Along with social respect and the Korean government's continued investment and reforms in education award teachers a variety of merits, such as competitive pay, job security, and better work environment (Center for Global Education, 2020; Center on International Education Benchmark, 2018). Obtaining a teaching position is competitive, and teacher education programs offer only a limited as well as selective entry for elementary school teachers. Although there are relatively more openings for secondary teacher education program, still only 20% of graduates can attain a teaching position in secondary schools. Such competition helps recruit the most qualified individuals to teach and promote a continuously enhanced school system (Center for Global Education, 2020).

The TIMSS survey data also revealed that a larger gap between schools with a lower level of violence and schools with a higher level of violence in U.S. schools, compared to Japanese and Korean schools. In the U.S., safer schools are more likely to have teachers who have the ability to inspire and have high expectation to for their students' academic achievement, active parental involvement, and students who have positive academic attitude and value peers' outperformance than schools with a higher level of violence. It is noticeable that level of parental involvement in schools with more violence in the U.S. reveals as the lowest (2.87 out of 5 points) across among all factors in across the three nations. As literature have demonstrated, parents in schools with experiencing poverty and violence problems are less supportive and less involved in students' academic performance. However, the gap of parental involvement in schools with low vs. high school violence is fairly large in U.S. (3.97 vs. 2.87), compared to those of Japanese schools (3.47 vs. 3.36) and Korean schools (3.84 vs.3.54).

There are several limitations of data analysis. Most of the literature on school violence utilize survey data or secondary data, which is limited to see cause and effect results. Therefore, we can see how certain factors are relevant to school violence, yet we cannot determine which the factors specifically cause the school violence in each instance. The analysis model mainly focused on school characteristics but rather than school culture and climate because it is the beyond the scope of this study. In addition, principals' reports on student problem behaviors are important for the research, yet data might include their prejudice and/or preconception. Students' misbehaviors can go unnoticed by adults and school principals might be unwilling to report frequent school violence due to potential damage of the school's reputations and being fear of losing support from communities (Klein, 2012). Lastly, this study is based on data of 8th grade students in Korea, Japan, and the U.S., and the results should be cautious to generalize to other different age groups.

References

Abdirahman, H., Fleming, L. C., & Jacobsen, K. H. (2013) Parental involvement and bullying among middle school students in North Africa. *EMHJ—Eastern Mediterranean Health Journal, 19* (3), 227–233

Akiba, M., & Han, S. (2007). Academic differentiations, school achievement in school violence in the USA in South Korea. *Compare, 37*(2), 201–219.

Akiba, M., LeTendre, G. K., Baker, D. P., & Goesling, B. (2002). Student victimization: National and school system effects in school violence in 37 nations. *American Educational Research Journal, 39*(4), 829–853.

Akiba, M., Shimizu, K., & Zhuang, Y. (2010). Bullies, victims, and teachers in Japanese middle schools. *Comparative Education Review, 54*(3), 369–392.

Cantor, D., & Wright, M. M. (2001). *School crime patterns: A national profile of U.S. public high schools using rates of crime reported to police. Report on the study of school violence and prevention.* U.S. Department of Education, Planning and Evaluation Service. Retrieved May 26, 2020, from https://www2.ed.gov/offices/OUS/PES/studies-school-violence/school-crime-pattern.pdf

Carlson, K. T. (2006). Poverty and youth violence exposure: Experience in rural communities. *Children and Schools, 28*(2), 87–96.

Center for Global Education. (2020). *South Korean education reforms.* Retrieved May 26, 2020, from https://asiasociety.org/global-cities-education-network/south-korean-education-reforms

Centers of Disease Control and Prevention. (2017). *School violence: Prevention.* Retrieved from https://www.cdc.gov/violenceprevention/youthviolence/schoolviolence/prevention.html

Center on International Education Benchmark. (2018). *South Korea: Teacher and principal quality.* Retrieved May 26, 2020, from http://ncee.org/what-we-do/center-on-international-education-benchmarking/top-performing-countries/south-korea-overview/south-korea-teacher-and-principal-quality/

Cho, R. M., & Choi, J. (2017). Social-psychological and educational outcomes associated with peer victimization among Korean adolescents. *International Journal of Behavioral Development, 41*(3), 329–340.

Choe, S. (2011). *In first, South Korea votes on social policy.* Retrieved May 26, 2020, from http://www.nytimes.com/2011/08/25/world/asia/25korea.html

Coley, R. L., Sims, J., Dearing, E., & Spielvogel, B. (2018). Locating Economic risks for adolescent mental and behavioral health: Poverty and affluence in families, neighborhoods, and schools. *Child Development, 89*(2), 360–369.

Dake, J. A., Price, J. H., Telljohann, S. K., & Funk, J. B. (2003). Teacher perceptions and practices regrading school bullying prevention. *Journal of School Health, 73*(9), 347–355.

Ellington, L. (2005). *Japanese education.* Stanford Program on International and Cross-Cultural Education. Retrieved May 26, 2020, from https://fsi-live.s3.us-west-1.amazonaws.com/s3fs-public/digest5.pdf

Ethem Erginoz, E., Alikasifoglu, M., Ercan, O., Uysal, O., Alp, Z., Ocak, S., Tanyildiz, G. O., Ekici, B., Yucel, I., & Kaymak, D. A. (2013) The role of parental, school, and peer factors in adolescent bullying involvement: Results from the Turkish HBSC 2005/2006 Study. *Asia-Pacific Journal of Public Health,* 1–13. https://doi.org/10.1177/1010539512473144

Frey, A., Ruchkin, V., Martin, A., & Schwab-Stone, M. (2009). Adolescents in transition: School and family characteristics in the development of violent behaviors entering high school. *Child Psychiatry Human Development, 40*(1), 1–13.

Georgiou, S. N. (2010). Bullying and victimization at schools: The role of mothers. *Educational Psychology, 78*(1), 109–125.

Han, S. (2010). A mandatory uniform policy in urban schools: Findings from the School Survey on Crime and Safety: 2003-04. *International Journal of Education Policy and Leadership, 5*(8), 1–13.

Han, S. (2014). School mobility and students' academic and behavioral outcomes. *International Journal of Education Policy & Leadership., 9*(6), 1–14.

Han, S., & Akiba, M. (2011). School safety, severe disciplinary actions, and school characteristics: A secondary analysis of the School Survey on Crime and Safety. *Journal of School Leadership, 21*(2), 262–292.

Holt, M. K., Kantor, G. K., & Finkelhor, D. (2008). Parent/child concordance about bullying involvement and family characteristics related to bullying and peer victimization. *Journal of School Violence, 8*(1), 42–63.

Hsieh, C., & Pugh, M. D. (1993). Poverty, income inequality, and violent crime: A meta-analysis of recent aggregative data studies. *Criminal Justice Review, 18*(2), 1993.

Jansen, D. E., Veenstra, R., Ormel, J., Verhulst, F. C., & Reijneveld, S. A. (2011). Early risk factors for being a bully, victim, or bully/victim in late elementary and early secondary education: The longitudinal TRAILS study. *BMC Public Health, 11,* 440.

Johnson, S. L., Waasdorp, T. E., Cash, A. H., Debnam, K. J., Milam, A. J., & Bradshaw, C. P. (2017). Assessing the association between observed school disorganization and school violence: Implications for school climate interventions. *Psychology of Violence, 7*(2), 181–191.

Johnson, S. L., Waasdorp, T. E., Gaias, L. M., & Bradshaw, C. P. (2019). Parental responses to bullying: Understanding the role of school policies and practices. *Journal of Educational Psychology, 111*(3), 475–487.

Kim, Y., Lee, S., Jung, H., Jaime, J., & Cubbin, C. (2019). Is neighborhood property harmful to every child? Neighborhood property, family property, and behavioral problems among young children. *Journal of Community Psychology, 47,* 594–610.

Klein, J. (2012). *The bully society: School shootings and the crisis of bullying in America's schools.* New York University.

Kramer, R. C. (2010). Poverty, inequality, and youth violence. *The Annals of the American Academy of Political and Social Science, 567*(1), 123–139.

Ladd, G. W., Ettekal, I., & Kochenderfer-Ladd, B. (2017). Peer victimization trajectories from kindergarten through high school: Differential pathways for children's school engagement and achievement? *Journal of Educational Psychology, 109*(6), 826–841.

Larsen, E. (2003). *Violence in U.S. public schools: A summary of findings. ERIC Digest.* ERIC Clearinghouse on Urban Education (ERIC Document No. ED482921).

Lee, S. (2007). The relations between the student-teacher trust relationship and school success in the case of Korean middle schools. *Educational Studies, 33*(2), 209–216.

Lereya, S. T., Samara, M., & Wolke, D. (2013). Parenting behaviour and the risk of becoming a victim and a bully/victim: A meta-analysis study. *Child Abuse and Neglect, 37*(12), 1091–1108.

Liu, D., Wong, S., & Roland, E. (2018). The family-school linkage in addressing bullying in Hong Kong: A sociocultural perspective. *Chinese Education & Society, 51*, 462–475.

Low, S., & Espelage, D. (2014). Conduit from community violence exposure to peer aggression and victimization: Contributions of parental monitoring impulsivity and deviancy. *Journal of Counselling Psychology, 61*(2), 221–231.

Lowe, K., & Dotterer, A. M. (2013). Parental monitoring, parenting warmth, and minority youth's academic outcomes: Exploring the integrative model of parenting. *Journal of Youth Adolescence, 42*(9), 1413–1425.

Milam, A. J., Furr-Holden, C. D. M., & Leaf, P. J. (2010). Perceived school and neighborhood safety, neighborhood violence and academic achievement in urban school children. *Urban Review, 42*, 458–467.

Musu, L., Zhang, A., Wang, K., Zhang, J., & Oudekerk, B. A. (2019). *Indicators of school crime and safety: 2018* (NCES 2019-047/NCJ 252571). National Center for Education Statistics, U.S. Department of Education, and Bureau of Justice Statistics, Office of Justice Programs, U.S. Department of Justice. Retrieved May 22, 2020, from https://nces.ed.gov/pubs2019/2019047.pdf

Näsi, M., Aaltonen, M., & Kivivuori, J. (2016). Youth hate crime offending: The role of strain, social control and self-control theories. *Journal of Scandinavian Studies in Criminology and Crime Prevention., 17*(2), 177–184.

Oh, K. (2013). *Korean teachers rank 4th in respect: Study.* Retrieved May 26, 2020, from http://www.koreaherald.com/view.php?ud=20131006000200

Organisation for Economic Co-operation and Development. (2018). *PISA 2015 results in focus.* Retrieved May 26, 2020, from https://www.oecd.org/pisa/pisa-2015-results-in-focus.pdf

Rekker, R., Pardin, D., Keijsers, L., Branje, S., Loeber, R., & Meeus, W. (2015). Moving in and out of poverty: The within individual Association between social economic status an juvenile delinquency. *PLoS ONE, 10*(11), e0136461.https://doi.org/10.1371/journal.pone.0136461

Ritchie, H., & Roser, M. (2019). *Urbanization.* Retrieved from May 22, 2020, from https://ourworldindata.org/urbanization#urban-slum-populations

Rubie-Davies, C. M. (2007). Classroom interactions: exploring the practices of high- and low-expectation teachers. *British Journal of Educational Psychology, 77*(2), 289–306.

Schuman, M. (2011). *What school lunches in Korea tell us about the future of the welfare state.* Retrieved May 26, 2020, from http://business.time.com/2011/08/26/what-school-lunches-in-korea-tell-us-about-the-future-of-the-welfare-state/

Shuval, K., Massey, Z., Caughy, M. O., Cavanaugh, B., Pilsbury, C., & Groce, N. (2012). "I live by shooting hill"—A qualitative exploration of conflict and violence among urban youth in New Haven, Connecticut. *Journal of Health Care for the Poor and Underserved, 23*(1), 132–143.

Thijs, J., & Verkuyten, M. (2008). Peer victimization and academic achievement in a multiethnic sample: The role of perceived academic self-efficacy. *Journal of Educational Psychology, 100*(4), 754–764.

Ullery, M. A., Gonzalez, A., & Katz, L. (2016). Mitigating the effects of poverty and crime: the long-term effects of an early intervention programme for children who were developmentally delayed and prenatally exposed to cocaine. *International Journal of Disability, Development and Education, 63*(4), 403–418.

Veenstra, R., Lindenberg, S., Huitsing, G., Sainio, M., & Salmivalli, C. (2014). The role of teachers in bullying: The relation between antibullying attitudes, efficacy, and efforts to reduce bullying. *Journal of Educational Psychology, 106*(4), 1135–1143.

Voison, D. R., Sales, J. M., Hong, J. S., Jackson, J. M., Rose, E. S., & DiClemente, R. J. (2017). Social context and problem vectors among youth with juvenile justice involvement. *Behavioral Medicine, 43*(1), 71–78.

Wang, C., Swearer, S. M., Lembeck, P., Collins, A., & Berry, B. (2015). Teachers matter: An examination of student-teacher relationships, attitudes toward bullying and bullying behavior. *Journal of Applied School Psychology, 31*(3), 219–238.

Webster, D. W., Gainer, P., & Champion, H. (1993). Weapon carrying among inner-city junior high school students; Defensive behavior vs. aggressive delinquency. *American Journal of Public Health, 83*(11), 1604–1608.

Xin, M. (2001). Bullying and being bullied: To what extent are bullies also victims? *American Educational Research Journal, 38*(2), 351–370.

Young-Jones, A., Fursa, S., Byrket, J. S., & Sly, J. S. (2015). Bullying affects more than feelings: the long-term implications of victimization an academic motivation in higher education. *Social Psychology of Education, 18,* 185–200.

Chapter 6
Individual and Family Characteristics and School Violence

While literature has shown various predictors of school violence and victimization from multiple perspectives, predictors at the individual level were revealed in a large body of empirical studies. Researchers have demonstrated that gender (being male), low self-control, low self-esteem, stress, depression, and lack of social skills are significantly related to student victimization and violent offending (Bowen & Bowen, 1999; Cho, 2017; Fox & Boulton, 2005; Lee & Kim, 2017; Organisation for Economic Co-operation and Development (OECD) 2018a; Walsh et al., 2016; Yang et al., 2013). Parental socioeconomic status is also an associated factor of student victimization and violent behaviors (Agnew, Matthews, Bucher, Welcher, & Keyes, 2008; Bae, 2017; Davis-Kean, 2005). In addition, experiencing physical harm caused by a family member as a child is associated with bullying behavior as either perpetrator, victim, or both (Dussich & Maekoya, 2007). Social relationship with parents, peers, and school teachers is well known as contributing factors in students' academic and behavioral outcomes (Crothers, Kolbert, & Baker, 2006; Harel-Fisch et al., 2011; Lee, 2007; Peterson, Lee, Henninger, & Cubellis, 2016).

In this chapter, major crime theories and previous studies were briefly reviewed regarding individual factors, family characteristics, and school violence. In addition, Korean students and their family's characteristics were explored and compared to the factors in Japan and the U.S. While quantitative studies are limited to interpreting cultural differences (Rutkowski, Rutkowski, & Engel, 2013), utilizing international data sets collected by nationally representative samples could be the best way to compare national indicators in a quantitative way. The Trends in International Mathematics and Science Study (TIMSS) 2015 survey data was used for this investigation. Specifically, students' gender, parents' education level, the extent of having educational resources at home, immigration status, language minority status, academic aspiration and achievement, and school attachment were compared accordingly with school violence in Korea, Japan, and the U.S.

© Springer Nature Singapore Pte Ltd. 2021
S. Han, *School Violence in South Korea*,
https://doi.org/10.1007/978-981-16-2730-9_6

Individual Characteristics, Family Characteristics and School Violence in Literature

Leading crime theories (e.g., strain theories and social control theories) explain that adolescents are more likely to become involved in delinquent behavior with the loss of positive stimuli (e.g., loss of relationship with peers) or the emergence of negative stimuli (e.g., unfair treatment and economic problems). Meanwhile, low self-control and low self-esteem are observed as strong factors of violence and victimization (Agnew & Brezina, 1997; Cho & Wooldredge, 2016; Udris, 2017; Yang et al., 2013). Data of 2,844 samples from the Korean Youth Panel Survey reveals that low self-control is significantly associated with peer victimization (Cho, 2017). Another Korean study based on 2,844 samples of 4th grade students found that low self-control and risky lifestyles including having delinquent peers are strong predictors of victimization (Cho & Wooldredge, 2016). Udris's study based on data of Japanese high school students showed that personal characteristics, such as low self-control and attitude toward violence, are positively associated with offline deviance. Social relationships have different impacts on students; meaning, attachment to parents and neighbors have a negative impact on offline deviance, whereas attachment to peers has a positive impact on offline deviance (Udris, 2017). U.S. national samples of 3,595 adolescents showed that relational problems with peers correlate with delinquency of both female and male adolescents, yet the correlates between interpersonal strain and delinquency tend to be more evident in male adolescents' delinquency (Agnew & Brezina, 1997).

Besides those factors in crime theories, many international comparative studies examined cultural factors in understanding violence. Given different frequency and severity of school violence across nations, researchers attempted to gain a better understanding of cultural differences (Benbenishty, & Astor, 2008; Bergmüller, 2013; Nesdale & Naito, 2005; Posick & Gloud, 2015). Collectivist and individualist cultures are the most distinguished cultural differences. Collectivist culture, commonly characterized in Eastern Asia countries, emphasizes goals/needs of the group, belonging, and harmony. On the other hand, individualist culture, characterized in Western countries, emphasizes individual's preference/desire, expression of individual's idea and privacy (Bergmüller, 2013; Gheorghiu, Vignoles, & Smith, 2009; Hofstede, 2011). Previous studies asserted that individualist culture tends to emphasize personal characteristics (e.g., self-control) for cause of violence, while collectivist culture tends to emphasize contextual and external factors for violent behaviors (Tyson & Hubert, 2002). Researchers have identified South Korea as one of the most collectivistic nations and the U.S. as the most individualistic, explaining that cultural background differently influences an individual's belief, attitude, and determinant of certain behaviors (Suh, Diener, Oishi, & Triandis, 1998). A study based on survey results from 62 nations reveals that cultural individualism is significantly associated with physically and verbally aggressive behaviors from students, after controlling for school and national factors (Bergmüller, 2013).

Gender differences are observed in many studies of school violence and victimization. A large body of research showed that a male individual is more likely to be involved in victimizing and violent incidents than a comparable female individual. Such a tendency is revealed in data from different countries with different economic statuses. Data from middle school students in 10 Asian-Pacific counties reveals that male students tend to report physical victimization than female students (Lai, Ye, & Chang, 2008). Data of adolescents in 19 countries in low- and middle-income households showed that more male students tend to report bullying (Fleming & Jacobsen, 2009). Samples of more than 2,900 Japanese adolescents (7th through 9th grade) showed that male students are more likely to be involved in bullying as bullies or victims than female students (Akiba, Shimizu, & Zhuang, 2010). Female students are less likely to commit deviant behaviors (e.g., frequently talking back to teachers, failing to comply to school rules, and using abusive language) than male students (Chen & Cheng, Liang, & Sato, 2012), and male students are more likely to commit delinquent behaviors than girls in institutional care systems (Ohara & Matsuura, 2016). In addition, Long and Dowdell (2018) found more victimization among male students than female (36% and 28.7%, respectively) from a dataset of more than 1,000 high school students in the U.S. With gender differences, there are also different forms of victimization. Physical aggression among male students and offensive rumor among female students were found as the most common forms of victimization from a dataset of more than 540,000 adolescents in 72 countries (OECD, 2018a). Male students are physically victimized twice as much and bully their peers three times as much than female students. Yet, male students are less likely to experience peer exclusion, as perpetuator or the victim, than female students (Akiba et al., 2010).

Age as an individual factor is also related to school violence, and a large body of studies examined delinquency and school violence among adolescents as such incidents occur more frequently in secondary schools than elementary or high schools (Agnew, 2003; Akiba, 2010; Chen et al., 2012; Musu-Gillette, Zhang, Wang, Zhang, & Oudekerk, 2017; National Center for Injury Prevention and Control, 2016).

Immigrant populations are growing around the world, and researchers are examining whether immigrant status influences school outcomes including victimization and school violence. Empirical studies explored that immigrant students are more likely to be afraid of attending school, are more vulnerable to victimization, and are more likely to have anxiety or depression than their non-immigrant peers (Bowen & Bowen, 1999; Ewert, 2009; Kim, Kim, & Kim, 2016; Peguero, 2009; Peguero & Jiang, 2014; Rojas-Gaona, Hong, & Peguero, 2016; Walsh et al., 2016; Watkins & Melde, 2009).

Socioeconomic status (SES) is a known strong predictor of violence and victimization along with family characteristics. Students having less educated parents and lack of resources at home tend to be physically bullied and excluded from the group by their peers (Akiba et al., 2010), and delinquent behaviors are more frequently observed among poor children in institutional care homes (Ohara & Matsuura, 2016). Data from 1,273 adolescents showed that self-reported delinquent behaviors (e.g., physical violence, vandalism, and stealing), drug use, and parent-reported aggressive behaviors are positively associated economic hardship. Specifically, adolescents who have negative experiences due to economic needs (e.g., postponed medical care or major purchases) are more likely to commit delinquent behaviors (Agnew et al., 2008). Such association is observed in international datasets. A positive association between socioeconomic inequality and social and physical violence is revealed in data analysis based on more than 269,000 4th graders and 261,000 8th graders in 52 nations (Contreras, Elacqua, Martinez, & Miranda, 2015).

School outcomes, such as educational aspiration and achievement, are significant predictors of bullying behaviors and victimization. Students who physically bully their peers are more likely to have lower academic aspiration and students who physically and verbally bully peers are less likely to value schooling overall (Akiba et al., 2010). National samples in the U.S. showed that low achievers, determined by reading scores, are more likely to fear school violence and more likely to perceive school as unsafe and tend to avoid participating in school activities due to possible attack or harm (Akiba et al., 2010). A comparative study revealed that low achievers in the U.S., determined based on mathematics scores, are more likely to fear being victims and to fear their peers' victimization. Academic achievement, however, shows no statistically significant association with those variables in Korea (Akiba & Han, 2007). An international survey data, based on more than 319,000 students, showed that approximately 43% of 4th grade students reported being bullied on a weekly or monthly basis. Those bullying incidents are significantly related to lower reading scores (Mullis, Martin, Foy, & Hooper, 2017). While the association between school outcomes and violence seems consistent, it is more apparent in some countries and not in others. A positive correlation between having difficulties in academic performance and being bullied was observed in five countries (e.g., Australia, Philippines, Singapore, Taiwan, and New Zealand), yet such a correlation was not evident in Korea and Japan (Lai, Ye, & Chang, 2008). Similarly, positive school experience, attitude, and perception significantly impact students' success in school. Many researchers explored the association between positive school experience and educational outcomes. For instance, victimization by bullies, having deviant friends, lack of positive attitude toward school, and lack of self-control of aggression are observed as factors of physical and verbal bullying (Akiba et al., 2010; Ando, Asakura, & Simons-Morton, 2005; Harel-Fisch et al., 2011; Kljakovic & Hunt, 2016).

Student Characteristics, Family Characteristics and School Violence in Korea

School violence is a critical social problem in Korea, and educators, parents, and policymakers try to ensure a safer environment (Kwon, 2012; Ministry of Education, 2017; Mullis et al., 2017; Yi, 2013). School violence causes emotional and physical harm and often occurs repeatedly to victims (Jang & Kwack, 2014; Lee, 2010).

Researchers found predictors of school violence and victimization from individual characteristics and family background in the context of Korea.

Being male has been observed as a strong predictor for being a perpetrator or a victim of school violence (Kim, Boyce, Koh, & Leventhal, 2009; Kobayashi & Farrington, 2020). A study based on nationally representative samples from the 2016 Korean Youth Risk Behavior Web-Based Survey showed that male students are more likely to have risk of violent victimization than female students (Park, Lee, Jang, & Jo, 2017) and data from 1,344 Korean students aged 10 showed that traditional bullying and cyberbullying are more prevalent among male students as both perpetrator and victim (Yang et al., 2013). Data of 756 middle school students in Seoul revealed that male students have a direct relationship between school attachment and low level of bullying, whereas an indirect relationship between peer attachment and low level of bullying was observed among both male and female students (You, Lee, Lee, & Kim, 2015).

It is well known that Korean parents strongly value schooling, support their child's education and are actively involved in their academic performance (Lee & Shouse, 2011; Park, Byun, & Kim, 2011; Seth, 2002). While parental support is important, its impact on adolescents differs by family structure and relationship between child and parent(s) (Cho & Wooldredge, 2016; Georgiou, Fousiani, Michaelides, & Stavrinides, 2013; Ohbuchi & Kondo, 2015). Data from 3,449 adolescents aged 15–19 shows that parental attachment is closely related to juvenile offense; when adolescents have increased attachment to their parents, they are less likely to be involved in bullying, fighting, robbing, threatening, smoking, and drinking (Lee, 2015). A longitudinal dataset from more than 3,600 Korean students revealed lack of parental supervision and lower grade point average (GPA) as strong factors of delinquency (Peterson et al., 2016), and living without parents is another indicator of victimization. There is about 16–25 times greater likelihood of being a victim among Korean adolescents who live with relatives or in a facility, compared to their counterparts who live with their parents (Park et al., 2017). Family structure is also associated with bullying; students who live with a single parent are more likely to bully their peers (Yang et al., 2013). Parents' socio-economic status (SES) and students' behavioral outcome were examined, and not only low SES but also high SES contribute to becoming victims. Researchers found that bullying is associated with low or high socioeconomic status among middle school students (Kim, Koh, & Leventhal, 2004), and the increased risk for bullying was found among adolescents with lower SES (Kim et al., 2009). Another study based on data from 64,020 Korean teenagers revealed that 23.19% of teenagers in high socioeconomic status are victimized, whereas 11.25% of teenagers in low socioeconomic status reported such victimization as well. Along with the descriptive statistics, results of logistic regression analysis showed that teenagers who are both in high or low socioeconomic status are more likely to have risk of violence victim (Park et al., 2017).

While parental factors are important, research shows that peer's impact on students increases, particularly for adolescents. As students grow older out of childhood, students' behaviors are increasingly influenced by peers than parents (Fleming & Jacobsen, 2009; Kljakovic, & Hunt, 2016; Smith, Madsen, & Moody, 1999). Peer influence might be greater in the Korean context because Korean students at the secondary school level stay for longer hours in school and even in cram school after regular schooling (Li, 2011; Park, Buchmann, Choi, & Merry, 2016; OECD 2018b; Peterson et al., 2016).

Although immigrant status is disadvantageous, it may cause more vulnerability in Korea (Kim & Kim, 2001; Kim et al., 2016; Lai et al., 2008). Not only because of cultural barrier, limited language ability, and different physical features, but also because Korea is an ethnically homogeneous society that tends to negatively view bi-ethnic and biracial adolescents and even reject them (Chun & Chung, 2011). Data from middle school students in ten Asian-Pacific countries showed that students with immigrant status and language minority status are more likely to be victims in Korea, Taiwan, Philippines, and Indonesia than the rest of the countries (Lai et al., 2008). In Korea, marriage migration (i.e., brides mostly from the Philippines, Vietnam, and China) has been encouraged by the Korean government since the 1990s, and it is a considerable contribution to Korea's rising immigrant population. As of 2014, a total number of multicultural families based on marriage migration is 24,387, and the number of bi-ethnic adolescents gradually increased from 9,389 in 2006 to 67,806 in 2014, 1.1% of the Korean adolescent population (Chang & Wallace, 2016; Kim et al., 2016; Statistics Korea, 2014; Lee, Lee, & Park, 2016). Online self-reported survey results based on 64,020 teenagers showed that adolescents with foreign-origin father or mother is more likely to be victims by bullying, threats, and even physical harm that require clinical or medical treatments (Park et al., 2017). Another study based on data from 3,627 bi-ethnic adolescents in the 2012 National Survey of Multicultural Families showed that about 8% of bi-ethnic students experienced school violence. In addition, among the victimizations, verbal assault is the most common form of violence and robbery and physical abuse is about two times more prevalent in male students than female students (21.5% and 22.1% vs. 10.3% and 11.1%). Male victims who report feeling indifferent about victimization are more likely to have depressive symptom than female students and students in other groups regardless of whether they seek or do not seek help (Kim et al., 2016).

Considering the competitive educational atmosphere in Korea, it could be assumed that academic stress is one of the strongest links to aggressive behaviors (Park, Choi, & Lim, 2014). Researchers examined how academic achievement is associated with victimization and violent incident and lead mixed findings. Self-reported online survey results showed that victims of violence are more common among high achievers than low achievers (23.3% vs. 17.4%) (Park et al., 2017). Victimization is related to low achievement; both to low and high achievement; or no meaningful relationship between academic achievement and violence and/or victimization (Akiba & Han, 2007; Park et al., 2017; Yang et al., 2013). There are many possible reasons for such inconsistency. For example, researchers assess academic achievement using standardized test scores, students' self-reports or teachers' reports and adopt different statistical analysis models with various control variables (e.g., family background, school environment, or personality). In addition, different types of violence (e.g., offline violence and cyberviolence) could be predicted differently. Data from 1,344 samples of fourth grade students from five elementary schools in Kwangju, Korea showed that low academic achievement is related to cyberbullying (e.g., sending intimidating or hateful emails/texts using the Internet), but there is no association between academic achievement and traditional bullying (Yang et al., 2013).

Comparison of Student Characteristics, Family Characteristics and School Violence in Korea, Japan, and the U.S.

Data and Analysis

To examine school violence, victimization, and student's individual and family characteristics, the TIMSS survey data was utilized. The TIMSS survey data has been collected since 1995, and TIMSS 2015 data was collected from samples of more than 580,000 4th and 8th grade students in 57 nations and 7 benchmarking entities (Mullis, Martin, Foy, & Hooper, 2016). In the analysis, samples of 8th grade students were selected as adolescent years have the most frequent delinquent behaviors during an individual lifetime (Agnew, 2003; Akiba, 2010; Musu-Gillette et al., 2017; National Center for Injury Prevention and Control, 2016). Data from 4,745 students in Japan, 5,309 students in Korea, and 10,221 students in the U.S. was used for the analysis, and each variable and measure for the analysis are presented below.

Variables

The TIMSS survey contains multiple questions about student's school experience and information about family background.

School violence is measured by student's responses to a question: "During this school year, how often have other students from your school done any of the following things to you?" Nine statements were given to students: "Made fun of me or called me names"; "Left me out of their games or activities"; "Spread lies about me"; "Stole something from me"; "Hit or hurt me"; "Made me do things I didn't want to do"; "Shared embarrassing information about me"; "Posted embarrassing things about me online", and "Threatened me." Students chose one out of four choices for each statement: 1 = at least once a week, 2 = once or twice a month, 3 = a few times a year, and 4 = never. This variable was reverse-coded and computed to use the mean of nine items in the analysis (Cronbach's Alpha = 0.81 in Japan, 0.77 in Korea and 0.86 in U.S.).

Students were asked "Are you a girl or a boy?" and chose one of the options. The TIMSS survey data includes 49% of male and 51% of female in Japan, 50.9% of male and 49.1% of female in Korea, 49.9% of male and 50.1% of female in U.S. This variable was recoded as female = 1 and male = 0.

Immigration status was assessed as to whether a student was born in the <country>. In the TIMSS survey data, students were asked "Were you born in <country>" and given choices 1 = Yes, 2 = No. This variable was recoded as 1 = No and 0 = Yes.

Language minority status was measured by asking students "How often do you speak <language of test> at home?" and students responded to always, almost always, sometimes, and never. In the analysis, students who speak the same language at home almost always, sometimes, and never were considered language minority students.

Parent education levels were measured by asking students "What is the highest level of education completed by your mother/father (or stepmother/stepfather or female/male guardian)?" and seven choices were given, ranging from some primary or lower secondary, did not go to school, and postgraduate degree. In the analysis, only bachelor's degree and postgraduate degree were chosen for education levels to compare across countries.

Home education resources were measured by asking students "Do you have any of these things at your home?" and given choice items. For the analysis, eight items were used including internet connection, own mobile phone, own room, and computer or tablet. Students responded to each item as 1 = Yes or 2 = No, and it was recoded as 1 = Yes and 0 = No. The sum of each student's eight responses was used for the analysis.

Aspiration was measured by asking students "How far in your education do you expect to go?" Students selected one from six choices ranging from lower secondary education to postgraduate degree. In comparison, only bachelor's degree and postgraduate degree were used.

School adjustment was measured by asking students five questions. Students were asked "What do you think about your school? Tell how much you agree with these statements" and five statements were given: "I like being in school"; "I feel like I belong at this school"; "I like to see my classmates at school"; "I am proud to go to this school", and "I learn a lot in school." Each statement was answered using a four-Likert scale ranging from 1 = Agree a lot, 4 = Disagree a lot. This variable was reverse-coded and computed to take the mean of five items for the multiple regression analysis (Cronbach's Alpha = 0.84 in Japan, 0.82 in Korea, and 0.80 in the U.S.).

Academic achievement was measured by the mean of five mathematics scores based on the TIMSS data. On average, mathematics scores are 585.76 in Japan, 604.06 in Korea, and 515.99 in the U.S.

Results

Figure 6.1 presents gender differences in victimization in Korea, Japan, and the U.S. The gender portions in the TIMSS data are similar across nations: 49% male in Japan, 50.9% male in Korea, and 49.9% male in the U.S. Victimization refers to students who experience violence (e.g., hit or hurt, made fun of, or threatened) at least once a week, once or twice a month, or a few times a year. Victimization was measured as the percentage of total number of victimizations out of total samples. Male victim

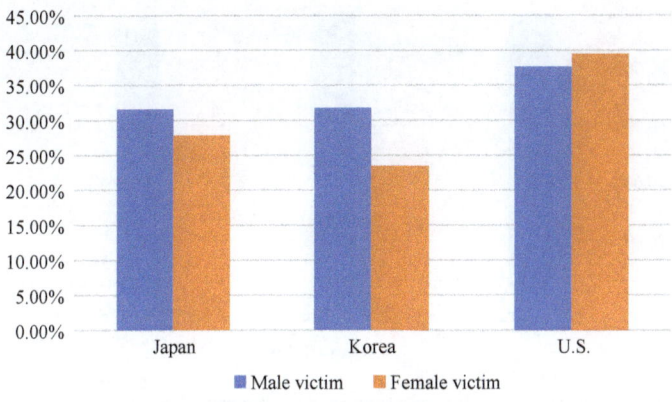

Fig. 6.1 Gender difference in victimization in Japan, Korea, and U.S.

refers to the percentage of male students out of total male samples. Female victim refers to the percentage of female students out of total female samples.

Overall, fewer Korean students are victimized by their peers compared to their counterparts in Japan and the U.S. (55.15% in Korea, 59.33% in Japan, and 77.05% in the U.S.).

It is noticeable that more than 77% of U.S. students reported being at least once victimized and there is a small gender gap, which shows prevalence of victimization regardless of gender. While more male students are victimized than female students in Korea and Japan, slightly more U.S. female students are victimized than their male counterparts in the U.S. Gender differences of victimization out of total samples in three nations include: about 32% of Korean male victims and about 23% of Korean female victims; about 32% of Japanese male victims and 28% of Japanese female victims; and 38% of U.S. male victims and 39% of U.S. female victims.

Figure 6.2 shows the percentage of 8th grade students who were born in the <country>. Almost all 8th grade students in Japan and Korea reported being born in the <country> (99.1% and 99.5%, respectively). About 94% of 8th grade students in the U.S. reported that they were born in the <country>.

When comparing the percentage of victimization by immigrant status (i.e., whether they were born in the country or not), different patterns are observed across nations. The TIMSS survey data shows that the percentage of students who reported being victimized by their peer at least once as 55.2% in Korea, 59.3% in Japan, and 77.0% in the U.S., respectively. Among victims, a majority of victims is the students who were born in the country; 99.5% in Korea, 99.1% in Japan, and 94.1% in the U.S. Fig. 6.3 shows percentage of victimization immigration status. Korea has the smallest percentage of victims with immigrant status (0.51%) and the U.S. has the largest percentage of such victims (5.94%). When examining the percentage of victimization among immigrant students, 55.6% of immigrant students in Korea, 61.1% of Japan, and 78.7% of the U.S. reported being victimized at least once at school.

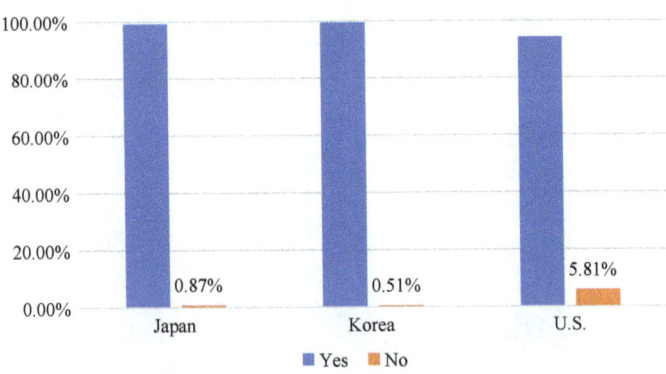

Fig. 6.2 Percentage of students who were born in the <country>

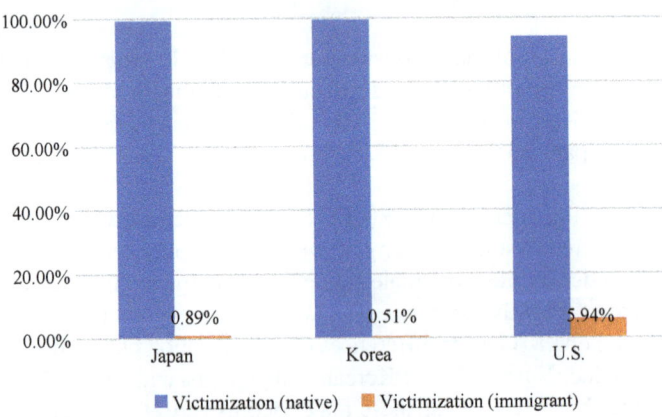

Fig. 6.3 Percentages of victimization by immigration status

Figure 6.4 presents the percentage of 8th grade students who speak another language at home, which defines language minority students in this analysis. Percentages of 8th grade students who speak the same language both at home and school appear to be about 96% in Japan, 89% in Korea, and 73% in the U.S. That is, 8th grade students who speak another language at home to any extent (always, almost always, and sometimes) appear approximately 4% in Japan, 11% in Korea, and 27% in the U.S. Because the U.S. has a more diverse population than Korea or Japan, the portion of language minority students is larger than Korea and Japan. Although Korea has been considered a racially/ethnically homogenous nation for a long time, it has recently changed to a more diverse population, and more than 1% of the Korean adolescent population comes from bi-ethnic families (Chang & Wallace, 2016; Chun & Chung, 2011; Kim et al., 2016; Lee et al., 2016). A recent Japanese government report shows that about 1.95% of foreign residents live in Japan. Overall, the immigrant population has been rapidly increasing in the past several years (Schreiber,

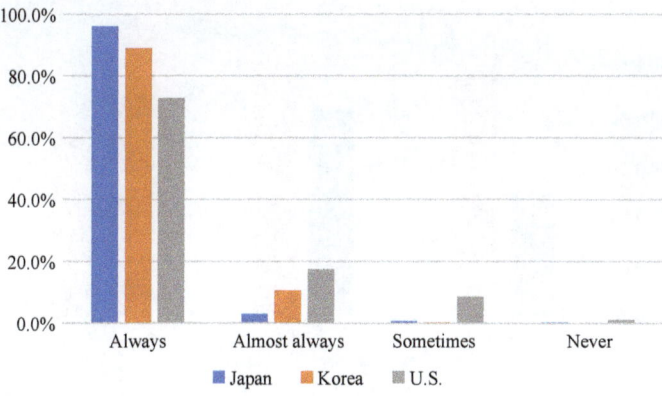

Fig. 6.4 Percentage of students who speak <language of test> at home in Japan, Korea, and U.S.

2018; Yoshida & Aoki, 2017), yet there is the smallest portion of language minority students among the three nations.

Figure 6.5 shows the percentage of victimization by language minority status in Korea, Japan, and the U.S. Korea has 13.6% of victimization with language minority status, 4.7% in Japan and 26.9% in the U.S. The U.S. has the largest percentage of students with language minority status, and it is more than five times larger than that of Japan. When examining the percentage of victimization with language minority status among those students, Korea has the smallest percentage and the U.S. has the largest percentage (67.6% in Korea, 71.0% in Japan, and 76.1% in the U.S.).

Figure 6.6 shows parents' education level, which was measured by choices selected on whether they had a bachelor's or a postgraduate degree. In Korea, more than half of 8th grade students reported that their father has bachelor's or a postgraduate degree, which is the highest among the three nations. About 41% of Korean 8th grade students reported their mother also has at least a bachelor's degree. In Japan,

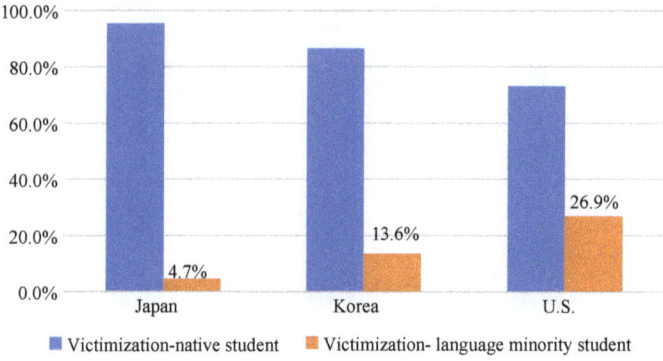

Fig. 6.5 Percentage of victimization by language minority status

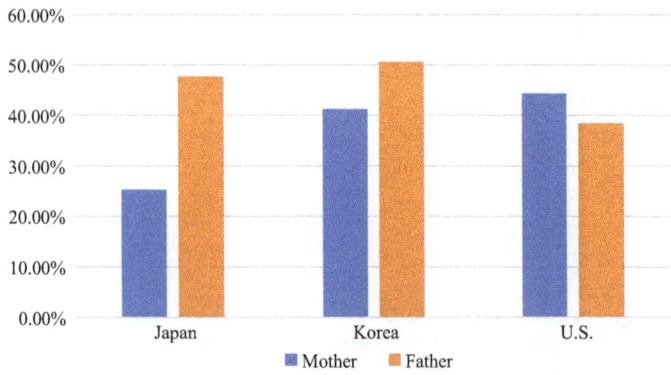

Fig. 6.6 Percentage of students having parents with bachelor's or postgraduate degree

about 48% of 8th grade students reported their father having a bachelor's or postgraduate degree, whereas only 25% of 8th grade students reported that their mother has such a degree. In the U.S, about 38% of 8th grade students reported that their father has a bachelor's or postgraduate degree and 44% of 8th grade students reported that their mother has such a degree. From the U.S. population, gender difference is quite small in terms of having a bachelor's degree (33% female and 32% male, see Ryan & Bauman, 2016), yet the current study shows that there is a larger gender difference for postgraduate degrees among U.S. parents having 8th grade students.

On average, a mother's education is the lowest in Japan and the highest in the U.S. In turn, a father's education level is the highest in Korea and the lowest in the U.S. The educational gap between the mother and the father is the largest in Japan and the smallest in the U.S.

Figures 6.7 and 6.8 show the comparison of victimization by parent's education levels. As Fig. 6.7 shows, on average, about 59% of victims in Korea has a mother without any degree, whereas it is 73.2% in Japan and 55.7% in the U.S. More than

Fig. 6.7 Percentage of mothers with have bachelor's or postgraduate degree

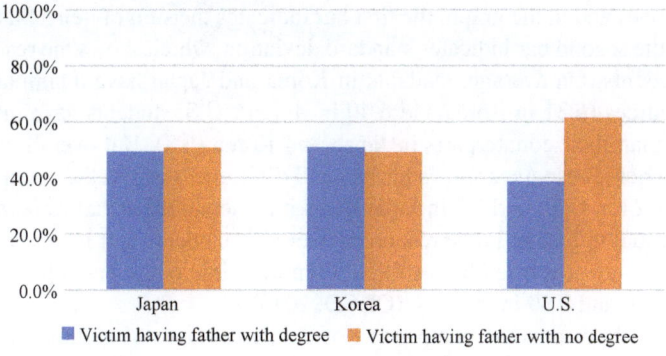

Fig. 6.8 Percentage of fathers who have bachelor's or postgraduate degree

half of victims in all three nations tend to have mothers without degrees, and this tendency is larger in Japan than in Korea or the U.S.

Figure 6.8 presents the comparison of victimization by father's education level. On average, nearly half of victims in Korea have a father without a bachelor's or postgraduate degree, whereas about more than half of victims in Japan have a father without a bachelor's or postgraduate degree (49.1% and 50.7%, respectively). In the U.S., more than 61% of victims have a father without a bachelor's or postgraduate degree. Students with uneducated fathers are slightly more likely to be victimized in the U.S. compared to their counterparts in Korea and Japan.

When comparing victimization by mother's and father's education, mother's education level is more likely to be linked to the victimization of an adolescent than a father's education level, which is more evident in Japan. However, a father's education level is more likely to be linked to the victimization of an adolescent in the U.S.

Figure 6.9 shows educational resources at home in three nations. Home resources were measured using eight items (e.g., Internet connection, computer desk, and

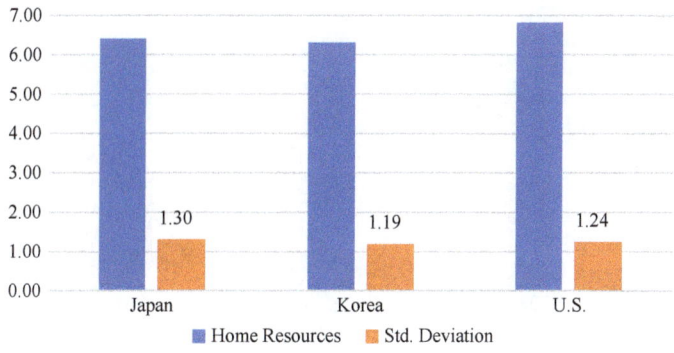

Fig. 6.9 Home resources in Japan, Korea, and U.S.

mobile phone) and in the graph, the first bar indicates the sum of items that students have, and the second bar indicates standard deviation, which shows the resource gap among students. On average, students in Korea and Japan have a similar level of home resources (6.31 in Korea and 6.40 in Korea). U.S. students have more home resources than their counterparts in Japan and Korea (6.8). But overall, the gap of possessing home resources shows fairly small differences across the countries (1.19 in Korea, 1.24 in U.S., and 1.3 in Japan), and it is inconclusive that Korean students are more equal in having home resources than U.S. students and Japanese students. . These results are supported by the OECD report; Gini coefficient is 0.30 in Korea; 0.33 in Japan; and 0.39 in the U.S. (OECD, 2018b)

Figure 6.10 presents the comparison of the percentages of victims by students' economic status measured by having home resources items. High status is having all 8 items, middle status is having 4 through 7 items, and low status is having less than 3 items. The largest percentage of victims in Korea is from the middle level of economic status (83%), while there are 62% in U.S. and 75% in Japan. While a majority of victims are at the middle level of economic status (63%, 75% and 83%), students having more home resources are more likely to be victimized than students having fewer home resources. The TIMSS survey data showed that the U.S. has more than two times the larger percentage of victims having high economic status than that of Korea. About 14.86% of victims in Korea come from high economic status, about 22.10% of victims in Japan, and about 35.94% of victims in the U.S. In addition, the U.S. has the smallest percentage of adolescent victims in low economic status (1.69%) with it being 1.84% in Korea and 2.60% in Japan.

Figure 6.11 shows victimization by students' aspiration, which is measured by the percentages of 8th grade students who wish to attain a bachelor's or postgraduate degree, in Korea, Japan, and the U.S. Overall, more than 60% of 8th grade students in all three nations hope to pursue higher education. Measured by being victimized at least once, about 74% of victims in Korea expect to have bachelor's or postgraduate degree, 61% in Japan, and 84% in the U.S. On average, victims in Korea are more likely to have an expectation for higher education than Japanese students, yet the largest portion of victims in the U.S has the expectation. Higher level of

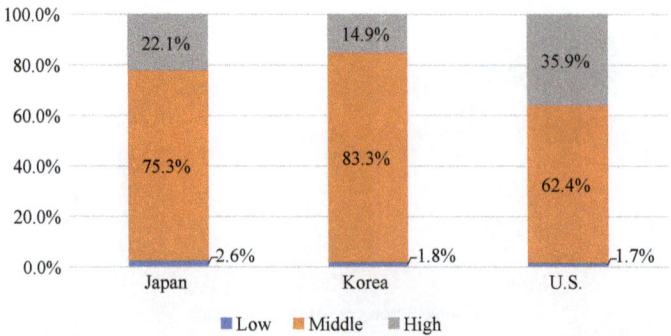

Fig. 6.10 Comparison of victimization by economic status in Japan, Korea, and U.S.

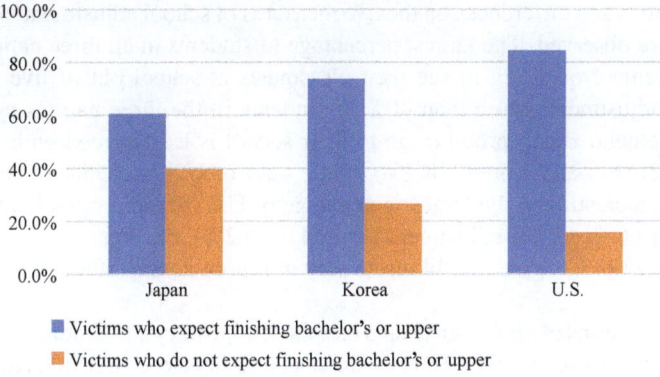

Fig. 6.11 Comparison of victimization by aspiration

academic aspiration in Korea and U.S. is also observed in an international survey result of Programme for International Student Assessment (PISA). Data of 540,000 adolescents showed that more than three out of four students in Korea and the U.S. expect completing university (OECD, 2018). The TIMSS survey data also showed that victimization in Japan tends to negatively impact pursuit of higher education than Korea and the U.S.

Figure 6.12 shows students' school adjustment in three nations. School adjustment was measured by five items, and each bar indicates percentage of students who responded to each statement as "agree a lot." Korean students are less likely to adjust school than their counterparts in Japan and the U.S. Less than a quarter of Korean students like being in school and less than 20% of students are proud of their school. Only less than 30% and less than 40% of Korean students reported that they learn a lot in school and feel belonging at their school.

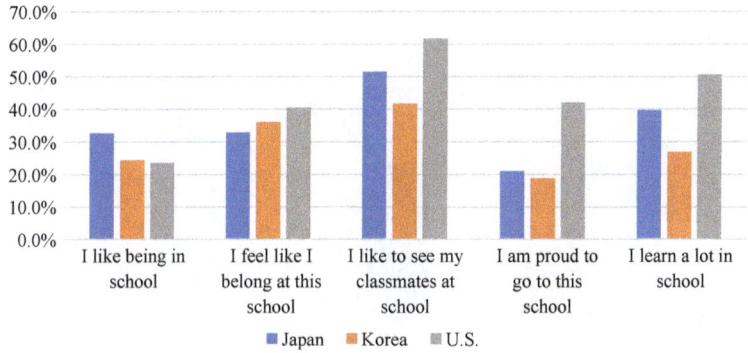

Fig. 6.12 School adjustment measured by five statements in three nations

Similarities and differences on the five measures of school adjustment in the three nations were observed. The largest percentage of students in all three nations agree on the statement of liking to see their classmates at school out of five measures of school adjustment. More than 40% of students in the three nations agree a lot on the statement. Being proud to go to their school is least agreed on by students in Japan (21.0%) and Korea (18.7%), while 42% of U.S. students agree with the statement. Interestingly, the largest percentage of U.S. students agreed a lot on the four measures on school adjustment (from 41 to 62%), the smallest percentage of U.S students (24%) agreed on liking to stay in school among students in the three nations.

Overall, in terms of all five measures on school adjustment, U.S. students are more likely to adjust to school than Korean students and Japanese students; responses to five statements ranged from 61.7 to 23.6% in the U.S.; from 41.7 to 18.7% in Korea; from 51.4 to 21.0% in Japan.

In summary, Korean students are less likely to adjust school than their counterparts in Japan and the U.S., and the findings are supported by prior studies. For example, a study of four countries from both Eastern and Western countries shows that Korean students are less likely to report misbehaviors than those in the U.S., yet they have significantly higher level of depression than U.S. students (Dmitrieva, Chen, Greenberger, & Gil-Rivas, 2004).

Figure 6.13 shows the percentage of students and victims who adjust well to school. Percentage of students who adjust well to school is 10.92% in Korea, 12.11% in Japan, and 11.76% in the U.S. Out of total TIMSS samples, only 4.49% of Korean victims report positive school adjustment, while 4.81% of their counterparts in Japan and 7.51% of their counterparts in the U.S. reported such adjustment. Overall, percentage of Korean students who well adjust school is the smaller in both total samples and victims, compared to Japan and U.S.

As Fig. 6.14 shows, academic achievement measured by mathematics scores showed the differences between non-victim and victims. In Korea, Japan, and the

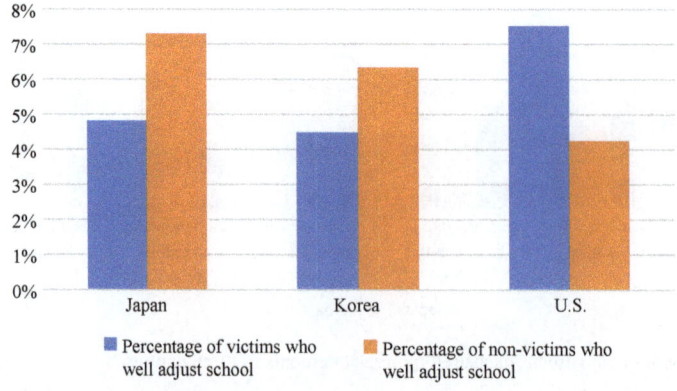

Fig. 6.13 Comparison of school adjustment between total samples and victims

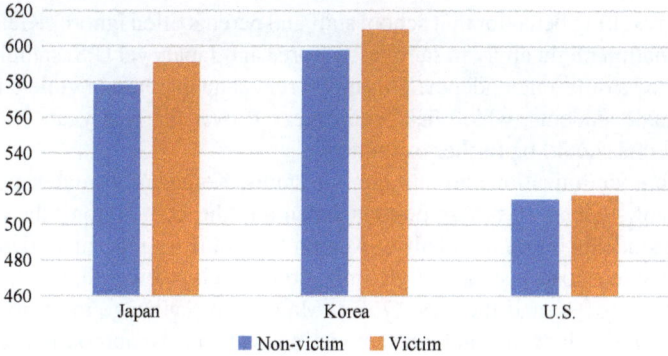

Fig. 6.14 Academic achievement between non-victim and victim

U.S., students who experience at least one instance of victimization have higher scores on mathematics. On average, Korean victims have mathematics scores of 609.44 and Korean non-victims have a score of 597.44, whereas Japanese victims are at a score of 590.99 with Japanese non-victims at 578.13. This finding is supported by a study showing high achievers' greater likelihood of being victimized than low achievers (Park et al., 2017). The math score difference between non-victim and victims is very small in the U.S. (516.56 vs. 514.08) (Fig. 6.14).

Summary

A large body of empirical studies has examined student's individual factors, such as being male, being of immigrant status, or a low academic achiever, are related to victimization and violence. In addition, family characteristics, such as lower level of parents' socioeconomic status and negative school experience, are more likely to contribute to student's victimization and violence. The findings based on nationally representative TIMSS samples in Korea, Japan, and the U.S. are helpful for understanding the patterns of students' victimization and their background. The findings are supported by many empirical studies, yet it is important to know that there are mixed results caused by different measures and analytical strategies.

Overall, student victimization is prevalent in Korea, Japan, and the U.S., and more than half of 8th grade students reported victimization in school in the three nations. Among the three nations, Korea has a smaller percentage of victimization than Japan and the U.S.: 55% in Korea, 59% in Japan, and 77% in the U.S. Gender differences are observed in three nations, and the gap is larger in Korea than that of Japan and the U.S. In Korea and Japan, more male students report being victimization than female, yet in the U.S., slightly more female students report victimization than male. It is widely known that male students are more likely to be involved in school violence. As many researchers argued, male students tend to earn recognition through masculine power, the resulting behavior that school staff and parents often ignore (Klein, 2012). This explanation might apply to samples in Korea and Japan, yet U.S. samples in this study showed a different tendency. This might reflect an increase in violent incidents among female students, which has been observed over the past years (See Klein, 2012), and this should be further examined.

Regarding victimization and immigration status, Korea has a smaller percentage of immigrant students in 8th grade than Japan and the U.S. Among the 8th grade immigrant students, more than half of Korean 8th grade immigrant students (56%) experience at least one instance of victimization, which is fewer than their counterparts in Japan (61%) and the U.S. (79%). Majority of language minority students who speak another language at home are victimized by peers; approximately 67% in Korea, 71% in Japan, and 76% in the U.S. from the total language minority student population in each country. According to the finding, a smaller percentage of language minority students are victimized by their peers in Korea than their counterparts in Japan and the U.S.

It is consistently observed in the three nations that victims are less likely to have parents who have bachelor's or postgraduate degrees than non-victims, yet victims are more likely to have educational resources at home than non-victims. Economic status has been an important but complicated factor in explaining school violence. This study used number of items of home resources to determine economic status and does not fully measure the extent and duration of poverty, which significantly influence life events (Agnew et al., 2008). To understand how economic factors are associated with school violence, there should be multiple assessments on economic status from different perspectives.

Despite limited measures, this study gives us an insight of how students' economic background impact victimization. Financial situation could help students to get along with their social group by possessing the trendy clothes and expensive electronic devices but at the same time having such things could be a target for victimization. In addition, a parent's higher social status including education level is essential for students to secure being an insider group (See Klein, 2012).

Another consistent finding across nations is that victims are more likely to pursue higher education than non-victims. The distinction of the pattern is more evident in the U.S. than Korea and Japan. This is interesting because victims might not be interested in schooling due to negative experience by peers at school. Nevertheless, victims are more likely to pursue higher education than perpetrators. In a similar way, higher score in academic achievement is observed among victims than non-victims in all three nations. That is, victims are more likely to be higher achievers and pursue higher education than non-victims in the three nations. The patterns here imply that students do not necessarily receive consistent recognition both by social status and intellectual achievement. At school, smart students are often harassed by their peers because of their academic success and/or lack of social skills (Klein, 2012; Park et al., 2017). Another interesting finding is that high achievers are more likely to be victims in Korea, Japan, and the U.S., yet the differences of the scores between victims and non-victims are very small in the U.S. On average, less than 12% of 8th graders strongly agree to multiple statements about school adjustment across nations. While non-victims in Korea and Japan are more likely to adjust to school, victims in the U.S. are more likely to adjust school. Current quantitative study has limits to explain this, yet it offers future research agenda on dynamic victimized students' strategies on adjusting to school.

References

Agnew, R. (2003). An integrated theory of the adolescent peak in offending. *Youth & Society, 34*(3), 263–299.

Agnew, R., & Brezina, T. (1997). Relational problems with peers, gender, and delinquency. *Youth & Society, 29*(1), 84–111.

Agnew, R., Matthews, S. K., Bucher, J., Welcher, A. N., & Keyes, C. (2008). Socioeconomic status, economic problems, and delinquency. *Youth & Society, 40*(2), 159–181.

Akiba, M. (2010). What predicts fear of school violence among U.S. adolescents? *Teachers College Record, 112*(1), 68–102.

Akiba, M., & Han, S. (2007). Academic differentiation, school achievement, and school violence in the U.S. and South Korea. *Compare, 37*(2), 201–219.

Akiba, M., Shimizu, K., & Zhuang, Y. (2010). Bullies, victims, teachers in Japanese middle schools. *Comparative Education Review, 54*(3), 369–392.

Ando, M., Asakura, T., & Simon-Morton, B. (2005). Psychological influences on physical, verbal, and indirect bullying among Japanese early adolescents. *Journal of Early Adolescence, 25*(3), 268–297.

Bae, S. M. (2017). The influence of strain factors, social control factors, self-control and computer use on adolescent cyber delinquency: Korean National Panel Study. *Children and Youth Service Review, 78,* 74–80.

Benbenishty, R., & Astor, R. A. (2008, June). *School violence in an international context: A call for global collaboration in research and prevention.* Presented at the IV World Conference: Violence at school: Violence in context? Lisbon, Portugal.

Bergmüller, S. (2013). The relationship between cultural individualism–collectivism and student aggression across 62 countries. *Aggressive Behavior, 39,* 182–200.

Bowen, N. K., & Bowen, G. L. (1999). Effects of crime and violence in neighborhoods and schools on the school behavior and performance of adolescents. *Journal of Adolescent Research, 14*(3), 319–342.

Crothers, L. M., Kolbert, J. B., & Baker, W. F. (2006). Middle school students' preferences for anti-bullying interventions. *School Psychology International, 27*(4), 475–487.

Chang, H., & Wallace, S. P. (2016). Migration process and self-rated health among marriage migrants in South Korea. *Ethnicity & Health, 21*(1), 20–38.

Chen, Y., Cheng, J., Liang, C., & Sato, M. (2012). Some factors in deviant behaviors of elementary school students in Taiwan and Japan. *Social Behavior and Personality, 40*(4), 623–638.

Cho, S. (2017). Self-control and risky lifestyles in context: Cross-level integration between opportunity and collective efficacy in the study of peer victimization among South Korean youth. *Journal of Child and Family Study, 26,* 67–79.

Cho, S., & Wooldredge, J. (2016). The link between juvenile offending and victimization: Sources of change over time in bullying victimization risk among South Korean adolescents. *Children and Youth Services Review, 71,* 119–129.

Contreras, D., Elacqua, G., Martinez, M., & Miranda, M. (2015). Income inequality or performance gap? A multilevel study of school violence in 52 countries. *Journal of Adolescent Health, 57,* 545–552.

Chun, J., & Chung, Y. (2011). A comparison of path factors influencing depressive symptoms in children of immigrant women and Korean children in South Korea. *Children and Youth Services Review, 33,* 2087–2095.

Davis-Kean, P. E. (2005). The influence of parent education and family income on child achievement: The indirect role of parental expectations and the home environment. *Journal of Family Psychology, 19*(2), 294–304.

Dmitrieva, J., Chen, C., Greenberger, E., & Gil-Rivas, V. (2004). Family relationships and adolescent psychosocial outcomes: Converging findings from Eastern and Western cultures. *Journal of Research on Adolescence, 14*(4), 425–447.

Dussich, J. P. J., & Maekoya, C. (2007). Physical child harm and bullying-related behaviors: A comparative study in Japan, South Africa, and the United States. *International Journal of Offender Therapy and Comparative Criminology, 51*(5), 495–509.

Ewert, S. (2009). Student misbehavior during senior year: A comparison of immigrants and the native-born. *Social Science Research, 38,* 826–839.

Fleming, L. C., & Jacobsen, K. H. (2009). Bullying among middle-school students in low and middle income countries. *Health Promotion International, 25*(1), 73–84.

Fox, C. L., & Boulton, M. J. (2005). The social skills problems of victims of bullying: Self, peer and teacher perceptions. *British Journal of Educational Psychology, 75,* 313–328.

Georgiou, S. N., Fousiani, K., Michaelides, M., & Stavrinides, P. (2013). Cultural value orientation and authoritarian parenting as parameters of bullying and victimization at school. *International Journal of Psychology, 48*(1), 69–78.

Gheorghiu, M. A., Vignoles, V. L., & Smith, P. B. (2009). Beyond the United Sates and Japan: Testing Yamagishi's emancipation theory of trust across 31 nations. *Social Psychology Quarterly, 72*(4), 365–383.

Harel-Fisch, Y., Walsh, S. D., Fogel-Grinvald, H., Amitai, G., Pickett, W., Molcho, M., et al. (2011). Negative school perceptions and involvement in school bullying: A universal relationship across 40 countries. *Journal of Adolescence, 34,* 639–652.

Hofstede, G. (2011). Dimensionalizing cultures: The Hofstede model in context. *Online Readings in Psychology and Culture, 2*(1). Retrieved August 26, 2020, from https://doi.org/10.9707/2307-0919.1014

Jang, H. J., & Kwack, Y. S. (2014). Psychiatric problems in the student victims of school violence and Their parents. *Journal of the Korean Academy of Child & Adolescent Psychiatry., 25*(4), 224–229.

Kim, Y. S., Boyce, W. T., Koh, Y., & Leventhal, B. L. (2009). Time Trends, Trajectories, and Demographic Predictors of Bullying: A Prospective Study in Korean Adolescents. *Journal of Adolescent Health, 45*(4), 360–367.

Kim, A. Y., & Kim, S. I. (2001). Comparisons of psychological factors related to school adjustment between children from international marriage families and from general families. *Korean Journal of Educational Psychol., 25*(4), 853–873.

Kim, J., Kim, J. Y., & Kim, S. (2016). School violence, depressive symptoms, and help-seeking behavior: A gender-stratified analysis of biethnic adolescent in South Korea. *Journal of Preventive Medicine & Public Health, 49,* 61–68.

Kim, Y. S., Koh, Y. J., & Leventhal, B. L. (2004). Prevalence of school bullying in Korea middle school students. *Archives of Pediatrics and Adolescent Medicine, 158*(8), 737–741.

Kljakovic, M., & Hunt, C. (2016). A meta-analysis of predictors of bullying and victimisation in adolescence. *Journal of Adolescence, 49,* 134–145.

Klein, J. (2012). *The bully society: School shootings and the crisis of bullying in America's schools.* New York University.

Kobayashi, E., & Farrington, D. (2020). Why do Japanese bully more than Americans? Influence of external locus of control and student attitudes toward bullying. *Educational Science: Theory and Practice., 20*(1), 5–19.

Kwon, D. K. (2012). 30% of children used violence against colleagues at school: survey. *The Korea Times.* Retrieved August 26, 2020, from http://www.koreatimes.co.kr/www/news/special/2012/10/139_122182.html

Lai, S., Ye, R., & Chang, U. (2008). Bullying in middle schools: An Asian-Pacific regional study. *Asia Pacific Education Review, 9*(4), 503–515.

Lee, C. (2010). Personal and interpersonal correlates of bullying behaviors among Korean middle school students. *Journal of Interpersonal Violence, 25*(1), 152–176.

Lee, S. (2007). The relations between the student–teacher trust relationship and school success in the case of Korean middle schools. *Educational Studies, 33*(2), 209–216.

Lee, W. (2015). A longitudinal study of victimization among South Korean youth: The integrative approach between lifestyle and control theory. *Children and Youth Service Review, 58,* 200–207.

Lee, Y., & Kim, J. (2017). An examination of victimization trajectories among a sample of South Korean adolescents: Risk and protective factors. *Crime & Delinquency, 63*(11), 1434–1457.

Lee, J., Lee, R., & Park, M. (2016). Fathers' alcohol use and spousal abuse and mothers' child buse in multicultural families in South Korea: The mediating role of acculturation and parenting stress. *Children and Youth Services Review, 63,* 28–35.

Lee, S., & Shouse, R. C. (2011). The impact of prestige orientation on shadow education in South Korea. *Sociology of Education, 84*(3), 212–224.

Li, A. (2011). South Korea cracks down on clandestine study groups. *Toronto Star.* Retrieved August 26, 2020, from https://www.thestar.com/news/world/2011/10/04/korea_cracks_down_on_clan destine_study_groups.html

Long, M. N., & Dowdell, E. B. (2018). Online and health risk behaviors in high school students: An examination of bullying. *Pediatric Nursing, 44*(5), 223–228.

Ministry of Education. (2017). *The survey of school violence in 2017.* Retrieved August 26, 2020, from http://moe.go.kr

Mullis, I. V. S., Martin, M. O., Foy, P., & Hooper, M. (2016). *TIMSS 2015 international results in mathematics.* Retrieved August 26, 2020, from http://timssandpirls.bc.edu/timss2015/intern ational-results/wp-content/uploads/filebase/full%20pdfs/T15-International-Results-in-Mathem atics.pdf

Mullis, I. V. S., Martin, M. O., Foy, P., & Hooper, M. (2017). *PIRLS 2016 international results in reading.* Boston College, TIMSS & PIRLS International Study Center. Retrieved August 26, 2020, from http://timssandpirls.bc.edu/pirls2016/international-results/

Musu-Gillette, L., Zhang, A., Wang, K., Zhang, J., & Oudekerk, B. A. (2017). *Indicators of school crime and safety: 2016* (NCES 2017-064/NCJ 250650). National Center for Education Statistics, U.S. Department of Education, and Bureau of Justice Statistics, Office of Justice Programs, U.S. Department of Justice. Retrieved August 26, 2020, from https://nces.ed.gov/pubs2017/2017064. pdf

National Center for Injury Prevention and Control.(2016). *Understating school violence.* Retrieved from https://www.cdc.gov/violenceprevention/pdf/School_Violence_Fact_Sheet-a.pdf

Nesdale, D., & Naito, M. (2005). Individualism-Collectivism and the attitudes to school bullying of Japanese and Australian students. *Journal of Cross-Cultural Psychology, 36*(5), 537–556.

Ohara, T., & Matsuura, N. (2016). The characteristics of delinquent behavior and predictive factors I Japanese children's homes. *Children and Youth Service Review, 61,* 159–164.

Ohbuchi, K., & Kondo, H. (2015). Psychological analysis of serious juvenile violence in Japan. *Asian Criminology, 10,* 149–162.

Organisation for Economic Co-operation and Development. (2018a). *PISA 2015 results in focus.* Retrieved August 26, 2020, from https://www.oecd.org/pisa/pisa-2015-results-in-focus.pdf

Organisation for Economic Co-operation and Development. (2018b). *Inequality and income.* Retrieved from http://www.oecd.org/social/inequality.htm#income

Posick, C., & Gloud, G. A. (2015). On the general relationship between victimization and offending: Examining cultural contingencies. *Journal of Criminal Justice, 43*(3), 195–204.

Park, H., Buchmann, C., Choi, J., & Merry, J. J. (2016). Learning beyond the school walls: Trends and implications. *Annual Review of Sociology, 42,* 231–252.

Park, H., Byun, S., & Kim, K. (2011). Parental involvement and students' cognitive outcomes in Korea: Focusing on private tutoring. *Sociology of Education, 84*(1), 3–22.

Park, M., Choi, J., & Lim, S. (2014). Factors affecting aggression in South Korean middle school students. *Asian Nursing Research, 8*(4), 247–253.

Park, S., Lee, Y., Jang, H., & Jo, M. (2017). Violence victimization in Korean adolescents: Risk factors and psychological problems. *International Journal of Environmental Research and Public Health, 14* (5), 1–11. https://doi.org/10.3390/ijerph14050541

Peguero, A. A. (2009). Victimizing the children of immigrants: Latino and Asian American students victimization. *Youth & Society, 41*(2),186–208.

Peguero, A. A., & Jiang, X. (2014). Social control across immigrant generations: Adolescent violence at school and examining the immigrant paradox. *Journal of Criminal Justice, 42,* 276–287.

Peterson, B. E., Lee, D., Henninger, A. M., & Cubellis, M. A. (2016). Social bonds, juvenile delinquency, and Korean adolescents: Intra- and inter-individual implications of Hirschi's social bonds theory using panel data. *Crime & Delinquency, 62*(10), 1337–1363.

Rojas-Gaona, C., Hong, J. S., & Peguero, A. A. (2016). The significance of race/ethnicity in adolescent violence: A decade of review, 2005–2015. *Journal of Criminal Justice, 46,* 137–147.

Rutkowski, L., Rutkowski, D., & Engel, L. (2013). Sharp contrasts at the boundaries: School violence and educational outcomes internationally. *Comparative Education Review, 57*(2), 232–259.

Ryan, C. L., & Bauman, K. (2016). *Educational attainment in the United Sates: 2015.* Retrieved August 26, 2020, from https://www.census.gov/content/dam/Census/library/publications/2016/demo/p20-578.pdf

Schreiber, M. (2018, Feburuay 17). *The face of immigration is rapidly changing in Japan.* Retrieved August 26, 2020, from https://www.japantimes.co.jp/news/2018/02/17/national/media-national/face-immigration-rapidly-changing-japan/#.WutJr4gvyUk

Smith, P. K., Madsen, K. C., & Moody, J. C. (1999). What causes the age decline in reports of being bullied at school? Towards a developmental analysis of risks of being bullied. *Educational Research, 41*(3), 267–285.

Suh, E., Diener, E., Oishi, S., & Triandis, H. C. (1998). The shifting basis of life satisfaction judgements across cultures: Emotions versus Norm. *Journal of Personality and Social Psychology, 74*(2), 482–493.

Seth, M. J. (2002). *Education fever, society, politics and the pursuit of schooling in South Korea.* University of Hawaii Press

Statistics Korea. (2014). *2014 statistics on the youth.* Retrieved August 26, 2020, from http://kostat.go.kr/portal/eng/pressReleases/1/index.board?bmode=read&aSeq=328722

Tyson, G. A., & Hubert, C. J. (2002). Cultural differences in adolescents' explanations of juvenile delinquency. *Journal of Cross-Cultural Psychology, 33*(5), 459–463.

Udris, R. (2017). Psychological and social factors as predictors of online and offline deviant behavior among Japanese adolescents. *Deviant Behavior, 38*(7), 792–809.

Watkins, A. M., & Melde, C. (2009). Immigrants, assimilation, and perceived school disorder: An examination of the "other" ethnicities. *Journal of Criminal Justice, 37,* 627–635.

Walsh, S., Clercq, B., Molcho, M., Harel-Fisch, Y., Davison, C., Rich Madsen, K., et al. (2016). The relationship between immigrant school composition, classmate support and involvement in physical fight and bullying among adolescent immigrants and non-immigrant in 11 countries. *Journal of Youth and Adolescence, 45*(1), 1–16.

Yang, S., Stewart, R., Lim, J., Kim, S., Shin, I., Dewey, M. E., et al. (2013). Differences in predictors of traditional and cyber-bullying: A 2-year longitudinal study in Korean school children. *European Child & Adolescents Psychiatry, 22*(5), 309–318.

Yi, W. (2013). 40% students suffer from school. *The Korea Times.* Retrieved August 26, 2020, from http://koreatimes.co.kr/www/news/nation/2013/01/113_128451.html

Yoshida, R., & Aoki, M. (2017, June 13). *Number of foreign students at public schools who lack Japanese language skills hits record high.* Retrieved August 26, 2020, from https://www.japantimes.co.jp/news/2017/06/13/national/number-foreign-students-public-schools-lack-japanese-language-skills-hits-record-high/#.WutMOIgvyUk

You, S., Lee, J., Lee, Y., & Kim, A. Y. (2015). Bullying among Korean adolescents: The role of empathy and attachment. *Psychology in the Schools, 52*(6), 594–606.

Chapter 7
Policy Implications from Comparative Perspectives

The Korean government made efforts to reduce school violence and promote a safer learning environment. In doing so, the Korean government established major school violence prevention policies in 2004, which include the antibullying law and a five-year plan. The policies emphasized protecting the victim and his/her rights and providing education and guidance to offenders to raise students as sound members of society. Additionally, the Korean government supported extensive research on school violence, therapy, and prevention education for successful policy implementation (UNESCO, 2017). In 2012, multiple suicide incidents of junior high school students revealed a severe and cruel bullying problem in schools, and it triggered the Korean government to initiate harsher antibullying policies. The Korean government deemed school violence as a social evil and established the Comprehensive Measure to Eradicate School Violence (CMESV) in 2012 (Kim & Oh, 2017). The CMESV policy stressed school violence as a social problem rather than the individual school's problem and provided seven practical guides: (1) emphasize school principals' and teacher's responsibility and roles, (2) improve system of report and investigation of victims and offenders, (3) expand school violence prevention education through peer activities and enhanced school culture, (4) increase parent education and parents' responsibilities, (5) stress a well-rounded education, (6) encourage parental involvement with social support, and (7) enforce the Internet games addiction prevention (Office for Government Policy Coordination, 2012).

Research on school violence from an international comparative perspective have been conducted by many researchers, yet little has been known about school violence in Korea, especially in its comparison to the U.S. and Japan. The three countries have compatible indicators in terms of economic status, students' academic performance, and national crime rates. Korea has been known as one of the fastest economically developing countries, and Korean students outperformed academic achievement in the mathematics and reading in the international assessments (OECD, 2020b). Japan has been known as one of the safest countries in the world with higher scores of gross domestic product (GDP), which is a major national economic indicator (OECD, 2020a). In addition, Japanese students academically outperformed in the international

© Springer Nature Singapore Pte Ltd. 2021
S. Han, *School Violence in South Korea*,
https://doi.org/10.1007/978-981-16-2730-9_7

assessments (OECD, 2020b). The U.S. is a country with one of the highest scores of GDP (OECD, 2020a). In addition, international assessments revealed that reading and science scores of U.S. students performed above averages among the OECD countries (though mathematics scores are below averages of OECD countries) (OECD, 2020b). School violence is influenced by multiple factors, and such different national context might offer insights to develop more effective school violence prevention policies.

This book has examined school violence in Japan and the U.S. in comparison with Korea focusing on (1) frequency and patterns of school violence, (2) perspectives of student, parents, teachers, and school principals toward school violence, (3) national characteristics and school violence, (4) school characteristics and school violence and the comparison of schools with low- and high-level school violence in three nations, and (5) student characteristics and family characteristics and school violence. To investigate these research topics, this book is based on data from mainly the Trends in International Mathematics and Science Study (TMISS) 2015, nationally representative datasets collected by the National Center for Education Statistics (NCES). Literature review was conducted based on selected studies published since 2000, and recent incidents and news articles were obtained from each government documents and major news networks. This chapter presents policy approaches to school violence, findings from this comparative study, policy recommendations as well as a future research recommendation.

Policy Approaches to School Violence in Korea, Japan, and the U.S.

The Korean government established school violence prevention policies by emphasizing comprehensive efforts involving parents and the community, and stressing school safety issues as a social problem. As mentioned earlier, the Korean government has various stakeholders involved in school violence prevention efforts and its improvement report and investigation system. In addition, Internet game addiction is included as one of the practices to reduce school violence (Office for Government Policy Coordination, 2012). While the Korean government initiated various violence prevention policies, there are little prevention policies on gender and sexual orientation minority students. Korea has been encouraged by the United Nations Committee on the Rights of the Child to include more content on sexual orientation, pregnancy, and gender identity in its school curriculum (Thoreson, 2019). Offering sexuality education at school is challenging because of traditional Confucius culture. Even if some schools offer in-depth sexuality education, it is not systemically developed, and the lack of professional instructors and disorganized content is not suitable to students' needs (Lee & Lee, 2019).

In the U.S., under the Student, Teachers, and Officers Preventing (STOP) School Violence Act of 2018, the federal government provides funds to schools and the local government to improve security systems, such as metal detectors and training programs (U.S. Department of Justice, 2019). Another national effort in the U.S. is the School Emergency Response to Violence (SERV) project. Since 2001, Project SERV (CFDA No. 84.184S) has funded various services for victims and witnesses to recover from violent and traumatic incidents and has also provided mental health assessments and improvements in school security. In 2015, under the Every Student Succeeds Act (ESSA), federal grant funds helped schools promote a supportive and drug-free school environment and various prevention programs, such as school-based mental health services, bullying or harassment prevention, counseling and mentoring for students, decrease of exclusionary disciplinary actions and trainings for school personnel to prevent suicide (Brock, Kriger, & Miró, 2018). Additionally, U.S. policies emphasize protecting lesbian, gay, bisexual, transgender, and queer or questioning (LGBTQ) students from being bullied and victimized at school. According to a recent national survey by Centers for Disease Control and Prevention, high school students are nearly two times more likely to be bullied than their counterparts because of their sexual orientation. About 33 and 27% of high school students who are lesbian, gay, or bisexual are bullied at school and in cyberspace, respectively, whereas 17 and 13% of their heterosexual peers are bullied in the same way (Kann et al., 2018). Gun-related violence at school is another critical issue in the U.S., and federal laws, such as the Gun-Free Schools Act and the Gun-Free Schools Zones Act, require schools to expel students who bring guns to school and prohibit any person from possessing firearm in school zones (Office of Elementary & Secondary Education, 2020).

In Japan, Ministry of Education, Culture, Sports, Science and Technology (MEXT) emphasizes school safety measures and develops a school safety system through active involvement with the local police and community to utilize more school guards for protecting students. In addition, there is a reform of education consultation systems by increasing school counselors and social workers to help victims of bullying and abuse (Ministry of Education, Culture, Sports, Science and Technology, 2020). In addition, schools are required to promote better understandings of sexual orientation and gender identity. Teachers are provided a LGBT guidebook to take necessary measures and respond to certain matters accordingly (Human Rights Watch, 2017).

In sum, each country has school safety policies with different emphases. All three countries stress community involvement to promote school safety and increase counseling programs and mental health programs for victims and offenders. The U.S. and Japan ensure policies that protect all students including those of sexual and gender minority from victimization, whereas Korea stresses parent education and responsibility for child's behavior and expands safety issues to prevention of online game addictions. In turn, with youth crime rates higher and more severe in the U.S., the U.S. government emphasizes security policies including metal detector at school and offering violence prevention training programs to school staff.

Findings from This Comparative Study

School violence in Korea, Japan, and the U.S. is compared with regard to the frequency and types of school violence by analyzing the Trends in International Mathematics and Science Study (TIMSS) survey data 2015. School violence is assessed by students' experience and school principals' reports. The TIMSS survey 2015 provides information about nine forms of school violence that students most commonly experience. It includes being made fun of or called names, being left out of the games or activities, having spread lies about them, having possessions stolen, being hit or hurt, being forced to do things, having embarrassing information shared, having embarrassing things posted online, and being threatened. School principals' reports on school violence are measured considering vandalism, profanity, intimidation among students, physical injury to students, intimidation of teachers, and physical injury to teachers. Students who participated in the survey are 8th grader in the three nations.

Data analysis of the TIMSS survey 2015 shows similar patterns and frequency of school violence in Korea and Japan, yet the U.S. has a larger percentage of student victimization across all nine forms of school violence. There are similarities and differences in school violence in Korea, Japan, and the U.S. In all three countries, the most common forms of school violence are being made fun of by others and having lies spread. Nearly half of the students in Korea and Japan experienced being made fun of by others. The percentage of students who are made fun of at least once at school for the past year is slightly lower in Korea (46.7%) than in Japan (48.1%), while more than half of U.S. students (57.4%) experienced being made fun of by peers.

There are fewer students who were victimized by having embarrassing things posted online, yet it is noticeable that U.S. students are approximately four times more likely to be victimized by this form of school violence than their counterparts in Korea and Japan. Another similar pattern is fewer students experience being threatened in all three nations, yet U.S. students are about three times more victimized than their counterparts in Korea and Japan. Among students who are victimized in at least one of nine forms of school violence in the three nations, more U.S. students are victimized in all nine forms of school violence, and more Japanese students were victimized by being forced to do things than their counterparts.

In Korea, over 60% of school principals reported that vandalism, theft, and physical injury are not problematic, whereas over 36% of principals reported intimidation and profanity as not a problem. These forms of school violence are reported by fewer Japanese school principals, except for intimidation, while the largest percent of U.S. school principals reported these forms of school violence as problematic.

The perception of various stakeholders on school safety-related matters was observed in Korea, Japan, and the U.S. Based on the TIMSS survey, data revealed students' perceived level of safety at school, teachers' perception of safety at school and the neighborhood, school security policies, and student's behaviors, and school principals' perception of students' violent behaviors toward students and teachers. In

Korea, about 20% of students agree a lot with the statement "feeling safe at school," and this is the smallest percentage among the three countries. On the other hand, more Korean teachers tend to agree on all school safety measures than their counterparts in Japan and the U.S. (except for one: student's behavior). Out of all the Korean principals' responses on six types of school violence, intimidation and profanity are the most common at school. In addition, Korea has fewer school violence incidents than the U.S., but more incidents than Japan, excluding intimidation among students and injury to teachers.

Approximately 43% of U.S. students agree a lot about feeling safe at school, which is the largest percentage of the three countries. Students who disagree a lot with the statement "feeling safe at school" are about twice more observed in the U.S. and Japan than Korea. A majority of teachers (more than 96%) in Korea and the U.S. perceived school as safe, whereas 88% of Japanese teachers responded in the same way. While more violent incidents were observed in U.S. schools, the largest percent of U.S. teachers perceived all school safety measures in a positive way. Feeling safe at school, school neighborhood safety, security practices, and students' behaviors are agreed on by more U.S. teachers than their counterparts in Korea and Japan. School principals in Korea, Japan, and the U.S. perceived intimidation and verbal abuse as the most common problems at school. Profanity was perceived by more Korean principals as a problem than Japanese principals. More than 60 and 35% of school principals in Korea and Japan, respectively, perceived profanity as a problem.

Overall, Korean teachers tend to agree with school safety than their counterparts in Japan and the U.S. While more students and teachers in the U.S. tend to agree with multiple measures of school safety compared to their counterparts in Korea and Japan, the largest percentage of principals in the U.S. reported school violence of the three countries. It is notable that perceived level of school safety in Japan appears higher than those of Korea and the U.S., except for violence toward to teachers. Approximately 35% of principals in the three countries reported intimidation and/or injury toward teachers as problems at school. On the other hand, in Japan, the percentage was reported to be twice that of Korea and the U.S.

National characteristics and school violence were compared in the three countries based on multiple international datasets and literature review. The six major types of crime were compared, and all three countries have higher rates of incidents in theft, burglary, and assault than rape, robbery, and homicide. Japan has the lowest, and the U.S. has the highest rates in all six types of crime among the three countries. Rate of theft in the U.S. is 1773.4, which is three and four times more than Korea and Japan, respectively. Burglary rates in the U.S. are 490.88, and this is three times and six times more than Korea and Japan, respectively. Assault rates in the U.S. are 237.57, and this is about more than two times and ten times than Korea and Japan, respectively. Spending on education and multiple economic indicators including employment rate was compared with violence/delinquency in the three countries, and Korea shows the largest portion of spending on education based on the percent of gross domestic product (GDP), whereas other national indicators are in between Japan and the U.S. The percentages of Korean students who feel unsafe in school become victims or experience teenage motherhood are the lower than those of Japan and the U.S. Overall rates of all indicators of violence/delinquency are higher in the U.S., and the teen pregnancy rate in the U.S. is more than 15 times higher than that of Korea.

School characteristics including poverty, school location, student, teachers, and school background were examined in regard with school violence. In the analysis, poverty was assessed by principals' report of percentage of students who are from economically disadvantaged families. School locations (from urban to rural) were determined by principals out of the five types of location, ranging from urban to rural. Teacher factors were assessed by the level of teacher's inspiration to students and an expectation for their academic achievement. The parental factor was assessed by parents' support and involvement in students' academic achievement. Finally, the student factor was assessed by each student's attitude toward academic performance. Results of data analysis revealed that 10.7% of Korean schools reported having more than 50% of students from economically disadvantaged families, whereas 1.4 and 43% were reported for Japan and the U.S., respectively. Approximately 30% of Korean schools have less than 10% of students from economically disadvantaged families, and 40% of Japanese schools and 15% of U.S. schools have students from economically disadvantaged families.

More than one-third of Korean schools (36.7%) are located in urban areas, whereas nearly half of Japanese schools (49.3%) are located in medium size cities or large towns, and 29.1% of U.S. schools are located in suburban areas. Compared to Korea, Japan and the U.S. are less likely to have public schools in urban areas; only 15.8% of Japanese schools and 22.4% of U.S. schools are in urban areas. In addition, U.S. public schools tend to spread across various locations unlike Korea and Japan. In the U.S., about 30% of schools are located in suburban areas, 23.8% in medium-size cities or large towns, 22.4% in urban areas, 18.8% in small towns, and 5.8% in rural areas.

Higher levels of teachers' inspiration for students and an expectation for their academic achievement, parental support and involvement in students' academic achievement, and students' attitudes toward academic performance are observed in Korea than Japan and the U.S. Korean school principals assessed the level of teachers' inspiration for students and having expectations for students' achievement as 4.37 points based on the 1 being very low to 5 being very high. Principals in Japan and the U.S. reported both under 4 points: 3.69 in Japan and 3.90 in the U.S., respectively. A higher level of parental factor, measured by their support and involvement for students' academic performance, was observed mostly in Korea. The parental factor was assessed by principals, and it was 3.59 in Korea out of 5 points, 3.41 in Japan, and 3.29 in the U.S. Lastly, principals' assessments on student factor (e.g., positive attitude toward academic performance and recognition toward peers' outperformance) were observed higher in Korea than Japan and the U.S. Korea was at 3.76 points out of 5, 3.53 in Japan and 3.49 in the U.S.

Regarding school violence, about a quarter of Korean and Japanese school public schools reported having no problem (25.3% and 24.5%, respectively), and only 12.3% of U.S. principals reported such response. There are consistent patterns on teachers', parents', and students' factors in regard to school violence; schools having a higher level in those factors tend to have fewer school violence matters in the three countries. Where teachers inspire students academically and hold higher expectation for students to perform academic achievement, there are less likely to be as many school violence problems. Comparison of levels between teacher factor and school violence are as follows. Schools with a lower level of school violence were assessed a teacher factor of 4.63, whereas schools with a higher level of school violence were assessed teacher factors of 4.27 in Korea. Similarly, in Japan, teacher factor was 3.92 in a lower level of school violence, and teacher factor in a higher level of school violence was 3.36. In the U.S., there are teacher factors up to 4.37 in a lower level of school violence and teacher factor of 3.62 in a higher level of school violence. Here, it is noticeable that the gap between the level of teacher factor and level of school violence is larger in the U.S. than Korea and Japan.

Regarding parent factors, the parental factor was assessed at 3.84 (out of 5 points) in Korean schools with a lower level of school violence and 3.54 in schools with a higher level of school violence. In Japan, the parental factor was assessed at 3.47 in schools with a lower level of school violence and 3.28 in schools with a higher level of school violence. Finally, in the U.S., the parental factor was assessed as 3.97 in schools with a lower level of school violence and 2.87 in schools with a higher level of school violence. It is interesting that U.S. schools have the highest points of parental factor in schools with a lower level of school violence among the three countries, yet U.S. schools have the lowest points of parental factor in schools with a higher level of school violence. Among the three nations, U.S. schools have the largest gap in the level of parental involvement between schools with lower and higher levels of school violence.

For student factors (students' positive attitude toward academic performance and respect for peers' achievement in schools) showed a link with the level of school violence. In Korea, student factors were assessed at 4.05 in schools with a lower school violence and 3.66 in schools with a higher level of school violence, respectively. In Japan, student factors were assessed at 3.69 in schools with a lower school violence and 3.36 in schools with a higher level of school violence, whereas in the U.S., student factors were assessed at 4.07 in schools with a lower level of school violence and 3.16 in schools with a higher level of school violence. Again, the gap between student factors and level of school violence is larger in the U.S. than Korea and Japan. According to principals' reports, Japanese schools have the lowest levels of teachers, parents, and students' factors among three nations, all below 4 points out of 5 (ranging from 3.92 to 3.28). For schools with both lower and higher levels of school violence, Korean teacher factors revealed the highest points out of the three countries. Such higher points in teacher factors are explained by traditional respect to the teaching profession and continued teacher education reforms in Korea. From highly competitive teacher recruitment policies to intensive teacher in-service programs, job security and other benefits that attract highly qualified young people to the teaching profession have resulted in an overall advancement in teacher quality (Center for Global Education, 2020; Center on International Education Benchmark, 2018).

Student individual factors (e.g., gender, immigration status, and level of academic achievement) and family background (e.g., parents' socioeconomic status) were examined in regard to school violence in Korea, Japan, and the U.S. The findings based on nationally representative TIMSS survey data in Korea, Japan, and the U.S. are supported by many empirical studies, yet it is important to know that there are mixed results caused by different measures and analytical strategies. The results showed that more than half of 8th grade students reported being victimized in schools in the three countries. Korea shows a smaller percentage of victimization (55%) than Japan (59%) and the U.S. (77%). Gender differences are also observed in three nations with the gap larger in Korea than Japan or the U.S. More male than female students report being victimized in Korea and Japan, yet in the U.S., slightly more female than male students report being victimized. As many empirical studies have demonstrated, male students tend to be more involved in violence, and they attempt to earn recognition through masculine power. Such behaviors are often ignored by school staff and parents (Klein, 2012). This explanation might apply to samples in Korea and Japan, yet the U.S. samples in this study show a different tendency. This might reflect an increase of violent incidents among female students over the past years (See Klein, 2012) and should be further examined.

Korea shows a smaller percentage of immigrant students in 8th grade than Japan and the U.S. Among the 8th grade immigrant students, more than half of Korean 8th grade immigrant students (56%) report being victimized at least once, and this is a smaller percentage than in Japan (61%) and the U.S. (79%). Similarly, fewer language minority students (i.e., those who speak another language at home) in Korea are victimized by their peers. Approximately 67% of language minority students are victimized by peers, while 71% in Japan and 76% in the U.S. are victimized.

In all three countries, victims are less likely to have a mother and father who have a bachelor's or postgraduate degree than non-victims, whereas victims are more likely to have more resources at home than non-victims. Economic status is one of the most important and complex indicators explaining school violence. As this study measured economic status based on the number of items considered resources at home, the actual economic status might not have been fully captured. The extent of and/or duration of poverty significantly influence life events (Agnew et al., 2008), and this should be applied to school violence research. Despite the limited measure of economic status, this study supports the link between victimization and financial status. Having a peer group and opportunities for socialization is especially important for adolescents. Forming a social group is often associated with possessing trendy electronic devices and clothes and helps being included in the insider group. Though interestingly, having such items is also the reason for victimization in some situations. Furthermore, having parents with a higher social status is another protection from being victimized (Klein, 2012). Investigating the relationship between violence and economic status among adolescents is challenging and calls for further research.

Lastly, students' academic aspiration and victimization show consistent patterns in the three countries; victims are more likely to pursue higher education than non-victims. The pattern is more evident in the U.S. than Korea and Japan. This is interesting because previous studies show that victims might not be interested in further schooling due to negative experience with peers at school. Nevertheless, victims are more likely to pursue higher education than non-victims. Similarly, more high achievers are observed among victims than non-victims in all three countries. Based on the TIMSS 2015 survey data, victims among 8th graders in Korea, Japan, and the U.S. tend to be high achievers and pursue higher education more often than non-victims. Some researchers explain that students might not receive consistent respect based on both social status and academic achievement. At school, high achievers could be harassed by their peers because of their academic success and/or lack of social skills (Klein, 2012; Park et al., 2017). Again, this finding needs more research to explain the link between school success, aspiration, and victimization. Another mixed finding from the previous studies is about the link between school adjustment and victimization. On average, about 12% of 8th graders strongly agree to multiple statements about school adjustment in the three countries. Non-victims in Korea and Japan tend to adjust school well, whereas victims in the U.S. are more likely to adjust school. A quantitative research like this study limits to explain this phenomenon, yet it offers future research agenda. Students' dynamic strategies against victimization could differ by their academic performance and attitudes in the three countries, and violence prevention policies should be developed accordingly.

Policy Recommendations

Data analysis of school violence in Korea, Japan, and the U.S. provides useful information and insight to improve school violence prevention policies.

First, school violence occurs in various form ranging from making fun of an individual to causing them serious physical harm. Severe violent incidents are rare, yet various emotional and verbal abuse are common among students in the three countries. School principals, teachers, and parents should pay attention to students' behaviors, interaction among peers and peer group, and there should be an increase of counseling programs for victims to get help from emotional, social, and physical harm from offenders. Not only victims, but also perpetrators should have adequate discipline and counseling programs to prevent further violence. Minor incidents are easily overlooked by principals and teachers, which might contribute to development of a negative school climate. In this study, victimization was measured by experience of at least one of the forms in a time frame, and there is no information on whether the students were victimized multiple times. Considering that repeated victimization of a particular student happens, incidents of school violence might be more prevalent than presented findings of the study. Schools need to be aware of the prevalence of school violence and take adequate precaution to prevent such incidents based on how many times a student experiences it in addition to how many students experience it ever. To promote a safe learning environment, proper support for victims should be offered. Discipline for perpetrators should likewise be implemented in a consistent manner.

Second, school violence is perceived differently by students, teachers, and school principals. Perception of school violence is observed differently by stakeholders and by form of school violence. Some incidents might go unnoticed or unreported due to lack of information or concern for the school image. For effective school prevention policies, all stakeholders should be informed of incidents and also frequent communication among stakeholders is helpful. It is possible for students, parents, teachers, and principals to define a behavior as violence or to casually dismiss it as a prank. Parents' responsibility for each student's behavior should also be emphasized, and parents need to be active in developing violence prevention programs as well. Parent involvement should be emphasized to promote a safe learning environment. Empirical studies show a strong link between parental involvement and prevention of school violence. When parents are actively involved in school events, those schools are less likely to have school violence (Lesneskie & Block, 2016; Wilson, 2019), and impact is more evident in elementary and middle school levels (Song, Quia, & Goodnight, 2019). Having a firm partnership between parents and the school has been well demonstrated as a positive factor for school safety, and it is one of the important keys for promoting safe school (Brubaker, Brubaker, & Link, 2001). School administrators should offer more opportunities for parents to become involved in school safety policies and discipline practices.

Third, there are similar tendencies in the three countries as schools with more students with positive attitudes toward academic performance, more teachers with the ability to inspire students with higher expectations of their students, and more parental support for students' academic achievement are observed to be safer schools. Schools where all stakeholders successfully play their roles have fewer violence incidents. This pattern proves that all stakeholders should be involved in the school prevention effort. Although the patterns are commonly observed in all three countries, the gap between a stakeholder's action and the level of school violence is fairly large in the U.S. That is, schools in the U.S. might have a stronger link between a stakeholder's actions and school violence than that of Korea and Japan.

Fourth, fewer Korean students and Japanese students reported cyberbullying (e.g., having embarrassing information posted online) than their counterparts in the U.S. Although cyberbullying appears as an occasional incident in the TIMSS 2015 survey data, usage of social media rapidly increases among students. Schools and homes should cooperate in developing prevention and intervention programs to prevent cyberbullying. Given the situation with increasing Internet use, school administrators, teachers, and parents should be aware of its negative impact on students' emotional and mental health. Cyberbullying could contribute to physical violence, and it is critical to prevent such situations.

Fifth, school administrators and teachers should be aware of vulnerable targets of violence and emphasize inclusive education. Data reveals that students with immigrant status in Korea are less likely to become victimized than in Japan and the U.S. Japan and the U.S. have a longer history for educating immigrant students and implementing multicultural education than Korea. Considering educational history in Japan and the U.S., Korea should stress the importance of multicultural education and implement a more inclusive curriculum that promotes a sound learning community.

Although the current study briefly addresses sexuality and gender minority students, school administrators and teachers need to be aware of needs for developing school violence prevention policies including LGBT students as well.

Recommendations for Future Research

Comparing levels of school violence among multiple countries is challenging because each country defines school violence differently. In addition, language and cultural differences might measure similar behavior differently, and researchers utilize data sources differently, such as self-report, school report, or police report (Shaw, 2001). This book attempts to examine school violence in Korea, Japan, and the U.S. The challenges in conducting international comparative studies on school violence have been reduced by utilizing nationally representative data, the Trends in International Mathematics and Science Study (TIMSS) 2015 survey data, collected from public schools internationally. In addition, the TIMSS survey questionnaire was translated using an internationally adoptive manner, which considers different education contexts and systems (Mullis, Martin, Foy, & Hooper, 2016).

While this book provides interesting information and insights for policymakers and researchers, there are several limitations.

First, quantified measures of school violence make the comparison possible across the three countries, yet there are still unexplained aspects. This book briefly presents different school systems, culture, and national characteristics in three countries. How those different contexts influence school violence is not fully addressed, and it is beyond the scope of this book. This calls for further examination on school violence embracing cultural context from an international perspective. Comparative perspective on school violence by integrating culture and systematic aspects is an important future research agenda.

Second, school violence needs to be explained from all stakeholders. This study had a lack of use of parent information, which is critical to prevention as well as intervention efforts. Information from community members and social agencies is also omitted in the study. Future study needs to utilize data from parents and the community to sufficiently capture the school violence phenomenon.

Third, the main results are based solely on the TIMSS 2015 survey data, and only 8th grade students in Korea, Japan, and the U.S. are selected for the data analysis. Therefore, it is unreasonable to generalize the findings to the entire student population.

Finally, research methods can be improved for future research. A mixed research method would be beneficial to explore school violence and cultural contexts from an international perspective. Measures of variables, such as violence and economic status, can be improved. For example, violence can occur multiple times and in various forms to one single student, and it should be counted as frequency of school violence. Economic status can be assessed using multiples measures including perceived financial difficulties. In addition, qualitative studies including case studies could provide deeper perception and reasoning on the current school violence phenomenon. Lastly, this study utilizes descriptive statistics, and future study could attempt relational analyses to reveal predictors of school violence. Examining associated factors with school violence in different education systems and cultural contexts would further aid our understanding of the school violence phenomenon.

References

Agnew, R., Matthews, S.K., Bucher, J., Welcher, A. N., & Keyes, C. (2008). Socioeconomic status, economic problems, and delinquency. *Youth and Society, 40*(2), 159–181.

Brock, M., Kriger, N., & Miró, R. (2018). *School safety policies and programs administered by the U.S. Federal Government: 1990–2016*. Department of Justice. Retrieved September 17, 2020, from https://www.ncjrs.gov/pdffiles1/nij/grants/251517.pdf

Brubaker, T., Brubaker, E., & Link, M. (2001). School violence: Partnerships with families for school reform. *Michigan Family Review, 6*(1), 1–11.

Center for Global Education. (2020). *South Korean education reforms*. Retrieved September 17, 2020, from https://asiasociety.org/global-cities-education-network/south-korean-education-reforms

Center on International Education Benchmark. (2018). *South Korea: Teacher and principal quality*. Retrieved September 17, 2020, from http://ncee.org/what-we-do/center-on-international-education-benchmarking/top-performing-countries/south-korea-overview/south-korea-teacher-and-principal-quality/

Human Rights Watch, (2017). *Japan: Anti-bullying policy to protect LGBT students*. Retrieved September 17, 2020, from https://www.hrw.org/news/2017/03/24/japan-anti-bullying-policy-protect-lgbt-students

Kann, L., McManus, T., Harris, W., Shanklin, S. L., Flint, K. H., Queen, B., Lowry, R., Chyen, D., Whittle, L., Thornton, J., Lim, C., Bradford, D., Yamakawa, Y., Leon, M., Brener, N., Ethier, K. A. (2018). *Youth risk behavior surveillance-United States, 2017*. Retrieved September 17, 2020, from https://www.cdc.gov/mmwr/volumes/67/ss/pdfs/ss6708a1-h.pdf

Kim, N., & Oh, I. (2017). Analysis of stakeholders' perceptions of zero tolerance policy for school violence in South Korea. *Journal of Educational Policy, 14*(1), 61–78.

Klein, J. (2012). *The bully society: School shootings and the crisis of bullying in America's schools*. New York University.

Lee, G., & Lee, D. (2019). Effects of a life skills-based sexuality education program on Korean only adolescents. *Social Behavior and Personality, 47*(12), 1–11.

Lesneskie, E., & Block, S. (2016). School violence: The role of parental and community involvement. *Journal of School Violence, 16*(4), 426–444.

Ministry of Education, Culture, Sports, Science and Technology. (2020). *FY2020 MEXT general budget highlights*. Retrieved September 17, 2020, from https://www.mext.go.jp/en/unesco/mext_00002.html

Mullis, I. V. S., Martin, M. O., Foy, P., & Hooper, M. (2016). *TIMSS 2015 International Results in Mathematics*. Retrieved September 17, 2020, from Boston College, TIMSS & PIRLS International Study Center website: http://timssandpirls.bc.edu/timss2015/international-results/

OECD. (2020a). *Gross domestic product (GDP) (indicator)*. https://doi.org/10.1787/dc2f7aec-en. Retrieved September 17, 2020, from https://data.oecd.org/gdp/gross-domestic-product-gdp.htm

OECD. (2020b). *Mathematics performance (PISA) (indicator)*. Retrieved September 17, 2020, from https://doi.org/10.1787/04711c74-en (Accessed on 04 June 2020).

Office for Government Policy Coordination, (2012). *Comprehensive measure to eradicate school violence*. Retrieved September 17, 2020, from http://www.opm.go.kr

Office of Elementary & Secondary Education. (2020). *Reports on state implementation of the gun-free schools act.* Retrieved September 17, 2020, from https://oese.ed.gov/reports-on-state-implementation-of-the-gun-free-schools-act/

Park, S., Lee, Y., Jang, H., & Jo, M. (2017). Violence victimization in Korean adolescents: Risk factors and psychological problems. *International Journal of Environmental Research and Public Health, 14*(541), 1–11. https://doi.org/10.3390/ijerph14050541

Shaw, M. (2001). *Promoting safety in schools: International experience and action.* Bureau of Justice Assistance. Retrieved September 17, 2020, from https://www.ncjrs.gov/pdffiles1/bja/186937.pdf

Song, W., Quia, X., & Goodnight, B. (2019). Examining the roles of parents and community involvement and prevention programs in reducing school violence. *Journal of School Violence, 18*(3), 403–420.

Thoreson, R. (October 16, 2019). *UN body urges South Korea to improve sexuality education.* Retrieved September 17, 2020, from https://www.hrw.org/news/2019/10/16/un-body-urges-south-korea-improve-sexuality-education

UNESCO. (2017). *School violence and bullying Global status report.* Retrieved September 17, 2020, from http://unesdoc.unesco.org/images/0024/002469/246970e.pdf

U.S. Department of Justice. (2019). *Student, teachers, and officers preventing (STOP) school violence program.* U.S. Department of Justice. Retrieved September 17, 2020, from https://bja.ojp.gov/program/stop-school-violence-program/overview#:~:text=The%20STOP%20School%20Violence%20Act,and%20prevent%20acts%20of%20violence

Wilson, A. (2019). The effect of community involvement programs on school violence. *The International Journal of Multidisciplinary Graduate Research, 1*(3), 1–11.

Lightning Source UK Ltd.
Milton Keynes UK
UKHW022211270622
405042UK00002B/6